五黄　星命
Five Yellow Life Star

Feng Shui Essentials: Xuan Kong Nine Life Star
FIVE YELLOW LIFE STAR

Copyright © 2011 by Joey Yap
All rights reserved worldwide.
First Edition July 2011

All intellectual property rights contained or in relation to this book belongs to Joey Yap.

No part of this book may be copied, used, subsumed, or exploited in fact, field of thought or general idea, by any other authors or persons, or be stored in a retrieval system, transmitted or reproduced in any way, including but not limited to digital copying and printing in any form whatsoever worldwide without the prior agreement and written permission of the author.

The author can be reached at:

Mastery Academy of Chinese Metaphysics Sdn. Bhd. (611143-A)
19-3, The Boulevard, Mid Valley City,
59200 Kuala Lumpur, Malaysia.
Tel   : +603-2284 8080
Fax   : +603-2284 1218
Website : www.masteryacademy.com

DISCLAIMER:

The author, Joey Yap and the publisher, JY Books Sdn Bhd, have made their best efforts to produce this high quality, informative and helpful book. They have verified the technical accuracy of the information and contents of this book. Any information pertaining to the events, occurrences, dates and other details relating to the person or persons, dead or alive, and to the companies have been verified to the best of their abilities based on information obtained or extracted from various websites, newspaper clippings and other public media. However, they make no representation or warranties of any kind with regard to the contents of this book and accept no liability of any kind for any losses or damages caused or alleged to be caused directly or indirectly from using the information contained herein.

Published by JY Books Sdn. Bhd. (659134-T)

Table of content :

1	**LIFE STAR REFERENCE TABLE**	7
2	**INTRODUCTION**	12
3	**YOUR XUAN KONG LIFE STAR**	23
	Basic Attributes	24
4	**YOUR FENG SHUI ESSENTIALS**	27
	Directions	29
	Taking the Direction using a Compass	33
	Favorable Directions	39
	Unfavorable Directions	49
	Bed Alignment Direction	58
	Best Floor	60
	Personal Grand Duke Direction	65
	Personal Clash Direction	71
	Flying Star Effects	76
5	**THE FIVE ELEMENT**	97

6	**CHARACTERISTICS OF STAR**	109
	The Good	111
	The Bad	117
7	**CAREER AND WEALTH**	123
	Characteristics at work	124
	Suitable Job Roles	128
	Career and Wealth Guide	132
8	**RELATIONSHIPS**	139
	Guide for Relationships	140
9	**HEALTH**	145
	Guide for Health	146
10	**COMPATIBILITY with OTHER LIFE STARS**	151

五黄 星命
Five Yellow Life Star

Year Pillar and Gua Number Reference Table for 1912 - 2055

Animal	Year of Birth			Gua Number for Male	Gua Number for Female	Year of Birth			Gua Number for Male	Gua Number for Female
Rat	1912	壬子 Ren Zi	Water Rat	7	8	1936	丙子 Bing Zi	Fire Rat	1	5
Ox	1913	癸丑 Gui Chou	Water Ox	6	9	1937	丁丑 Ding Chou	Fire Ox	9	6
Tiger	1914	甲寅 Jia Yin	Wood Tiger	5	1	1938	戊寅 Wu Yin	Earth Tiger	8	7
Rabbit	1915	乙卯 Yi Mao	Wood Rabbit	4	2	1939	己卯 Ji Mao	Earth Rabbit	7	8
Dragon	1916	丙辰 Bing Chen	Fire Dragon	3	3	1940	庚辰 Geng Chen	Metal Dragon	6	9
Snake	1917	丁巳 Ding Si	Fire Snake	2	4	1941	辛巳 Xin Si	Metal Snake	5	1
Horse	1918	戊午 Wu Wu	Earth Horse	1	5	1942	壬午 Ren Wu	Water Horse	4	2
Goat	1919	己未 Ji Wei	Earth Goat	9	6	1943	癸未 Gui Wei	Water Goat	3	3
Monkey	1920	庚申 Geng Shen	Metal Monkey	8	7	1944	甲申 Jia Shen	Wood Monkey	2	4
Rooster	1921	辛酉 Xin You	Metal Rooster	7	8	1945	乙酉 Yi You	Wood Rooster	1	5
Dog	1922	壬戌 Ren Xu	Water Dog	6	9	1946	丙戌 Bing Xu	Fire Dog	9	6
Pig	1923	癸亥 Gui Hai	Water Pig	5	1	1947	丁亥 Ding Hai	Fire Pig	8	7
Rat	1924	甲子 Jia Zi	Wood Rat	4	2	1948	戊子 Wu Zi	Earth Rat	7	8
Ox	1925	乙丑 Yi Chou	Wood Ox	3	3	1949	己丑 Ji Chou	Earth Ox	6	9
Tiger	1926	丙寅 Bing Yin	Fire Tiger	2	4	1950	庚寅 Geng Yin	Metal Tiger	5	1
Rabbit	1927	丁卯 Ding Mao	Fire Rabbit	1	5	1951	辛卯 Xin Mao	Metal Rabbit	4	2
Dragon	1928	戊辰 Wu Chen	Earth Dragon	9	6	1952	壬辰 Ren Chen	Water Dragon	3	3
Snake	1929	己巳 Ji Si	Earth Snake	8	7	1953	癸巳 Gui Si	Water Snake	2	4
Horse	1930	庚午 Geng Wu	Metal Horse	7	8	1954	甲午 Jia Wu	Wood Horse	1	5
Goat	1931	辛未 Xin Wei	Metal Goat	6	9	1955	乙未 Yi Wei	Wood Goat	9	6
Monkey	1932	壬申 Ren Shen	Water Monkey	5	1	1956	丙申 Bing Shen	Fire Monkey	8	7
Rooster	1933	癸酉 Gui You	Water Rooster	4	2	1957	丁酉 Ding You	Fire Rooster	7	8
Dog	1934	甲戌 Jia Xu	Wood Dog	3	3	1958	戊戌 Wu Xu	Earth Dog	6	9
Pig	1935	乙亥 Yi Hai	Wood Pig	2	4	1959	己亥 Ji Hai	Earth Pig	5	1

- Please note that the date for the Chinese Solar Year starts on Feb 4. This means that if you were born in Feb 2 of 2002, you belong to the previous year 2001.

Year Pillar and Gua Number Reference Table for 1912 - 2055

Animal	Year of Birth			Gua Number for Male	Gua Number for Female	Year of Birth			Gua Number for Male	Gua Number for Female
Rat	1960	庚子 Geng Zi	Metal Rat	4	2	1984	甲子 Jia Zi	Wood Rat	7	8
Ox	1961	辛丑 Xin Chou	Metal Ox	3	3	1985	乙丑 Yi Chou	Wood Ox	6	9
Tiger	1962	壬寅 Ren Yin	Water Tiger	2	4	1986	丙寅 Bing Yin	Fire Tiger	5	1
Rabbit	1963	癸卯 Gui Mao	Water Rabbit	1	5	1987	丁卯 Ding Mao	Fire Rabbit	4	2
Dragon	1964	甲辰 Jia Chen	Wood Dragon	9	6	1988	戊辰 Wu Chen	Earth Dragon	3	3
Snake	1965	乙巳 Yi Si	Wood Snake	8	7	1989	己巳 Ji Si	Earth Snake	2	4
Horse	1966	丙午 Bing Wu	Fire Horse	7	8	1990	庚午 Geng Wu	Metal Horse	1	5
Goat	1967	丁未 Ding Wei	Fire Goat	6	9	1991	辛未 Xin Wei	Metal Goat	9	6
Monkey	1968	戊申 Wu Shen	Earth Monkey	5	1	1992	壬申 Ren Shen	Water Monkey	8	7
Rooster	1969	己酉 Ji You	Earth Rooster	4	2	1993	癸酉 Gui You	Water Rooster	7	8
Dog	1970	庚戌 Geng Xu	Metal Dog	3	3	1994	甲戌 Jia Xu	Wood Dog	6	9
Pig	1971	辛亥 Xin Hai	Metal Pig	2	4	1995	乙亥 Yi Hai	Wood Pig	5	1
Rat	1972	壬子 Ren Zi	Water Rat	1	5	1996	丙子 Bing Zi	Fire Rat	4	2
Ox	1973	癸丑 Gui Chou	Water Ox	9	6	1997	丁丑 Ding Chou	Fire Ox	3	3
Tiger	1974	甲寅 Jia Yin	Wood Tiger	8	7	1998	戊寅 Wu Yin	Earth Tiger	2	4
Rabbit	1975	乙卯 Yi Mao	Wood Rabbit	7	8	1999	己卯 Ji Mao	Earth Rabbit	1	5
Dragon	1976	丙辰 Bing Chen	Fire Dragon	6	9	2000	庚辰 Geng Chen	Metal Dragon	9	6
Snake	1977	丁巳 Ding Si	Fire Snake	5	1	2001	辛巳 Xin Si	Metal Snake	8	7
Horse	1978	戊午 Wu Wu	Earth Horse	4	2	2002	壬午 Ren Wu	Water Horse	7	8
Goat	1979	己未 Ji Wei	Earth Goat	3	3	2003	癸未 Gui Wei	Water Goat	6	9
Monkey	1980	庚申 Geng Shen	Metal Monkey	2	4	2004	甲申 Jia Shen	Wood Monkey	5	1
Rooster	1981	辛酉 Xin You	Metal Rooster	1	5	2005	乙酉 Yi You	Wood Rooster	4	2
Dog	1982	壬戌 Ren Xu	Water Dog	9	6	2006	丙戌 Bing Xu	Fire Dog	3	3
Pig	1983	癸亥 Gui Hai	Water Pig	8	7	2007	丁亥 Ding Hai	Fire Pig	2	4

- Please note that the date for the Chinese Solar Year starts on Feb 4. This means that if you were born in Feb 2 of 2002, you belong to the previous year 2001.

Year Pillar and Gua Number Reference Table for 1912 - 2055

Animal	Year of Birth			Gua Number for Male	Gua Number for Female	Year of Birth			Gua Number for Male	Gua Number for Female
Rat	2008	戊子 Wu Zi	Earth Rat	1	5	2032	壬子 Ren Zi	Water Rat	4	2
Ox	2009	己丑 Ji Chou	Earth Ox	9	6	2033	癸丑 Gui Chou	Water Ox	3	3
Tiger	2010	庚寅 Geng Yin	Metal Tiger	8	7	2034	甲寅 Jia Yin	Wood Tiger	2	4
Rabbit	2011	辛卯 Xin Mao	Metal Rabbit	7	8	2035	乙卯 Yi Mao	Wood Rabbit	1	5
Dragon	2012	壬辰 Ren Chen	Water Dragon	6	9	2036	丙辰 Bing Chen	Fire Dragon	9	6
Snake	2013	癸巳 Gui Si	Water Snake	5	1	2037	丁巳 Ding Si	Fire Snake	8	7
Horse	2014	甲午 Jia Wu	Wood Horse	4	2	2038	戊午 Wu Wu	Earth Horse	7	8
Goat	2015	乙未 Yi Wei	Wood Goat	3	3	2039	己未 Ji Wei	Earth Goat	6	9
Monkey	2016	丙申 Bing Shen	Fire Monkey	2	4	2040	庚申 Geng Shen	Metal Monkey	5	1
Rooster	2017	丁酉 Ding You	Fire Rooster	1	5	2041	辛酉 Xin You	Metal Rooster	4	2
Dog	2018	戊戌 Wu Xu	Earth Dog	9	6	2042	壬戌 Ren Xu	Water Dog	3	3
Pig	2019	己亥 Ji Hai	Earth Pig	8	7	2043	癸亥 Gui Hai	Water Pig	2	4
Rat	2020	庚子 Geng Zi	Metal Rat	7	8	2044	甲子 Jia Zi	Wood Rat	1	5
Ox	2021	辛丑 Xin Chou	Metal Ox	6	9	2045	乙丑 Yi Chou	Wood Ox	9	6
Tiger	2022	壬寅 Ren Yin	Water Tiger	5	1	2046	丙寅 Bing Yin	Fire Tiger	8	7
Rabbit	2023	癸卯 Gui Mao	Water Rabbit	4	2	2047	丁卯 Ding Mao	Fire Rabbit	7	8
Dragon	2024	甲辰 Jia Chen	Wood Dragon	3	3	2048	戊辰 Wu Chen	Earth Dragon	6	9
Snake	2025	乙巳 Yi Si	Wood Snake	2	4	2049	己巳 Ji Si	Earth Snake	5	1
Horse	2026	丙午 Bing Wu	Fire Horse	1	5	2050	庚午 Geng Wu	Metal Horse	4	2
Goat	2027	丁未 Ding Wei	Fire Goat	9	6	2051	辛未 Xin Wei	Metal Goat	3	3
Monkey	2028	戊申 Wu Shen	Earth Monkey	8	7	2052	壬申 Ren Shen	Water Monkey	2	4
Rooster	2029	己酉 Ji You	Earth Rooster	7	8	2053	癸酉 Gui You	Water Rooster	1	5
Dog	2030	庚戌 Geng Xu	Metal Dog	6	9	2054	甲戌 Jia Xu	Wood Dog	9	6
Pig	2031	辛亥 Xin Hai	Metal Pig	5	1	2055	乙亥 Yi Hai	Wood Pig	8	7

- Please note that the date for the Chinese Solar Year starts on Feb 4. This means that if you were born in Feb 2 of 2002, you belong to the previous year 2001.

To download your Five Yellow Life Star Reference Chart FREE go to

www.masteryacademy.com/regbook

Here is your unique code for access:

GBSN6015

Introduction

When all is said and done, Feng Shui is the study of how environments affect the people living within them. It can yield advice on which environments, at both a macro and micro level, are 'good' places or 'bad' places to live for given people at given times.

Xuan Kong is only one subsection of the study of Feng Shui and the Life Stars are only one component in the Xuan Kong Feng Shui system. This means that the study of Life Stars gives us only one piece of the overall Feng Shui puzzle but it is an important one!

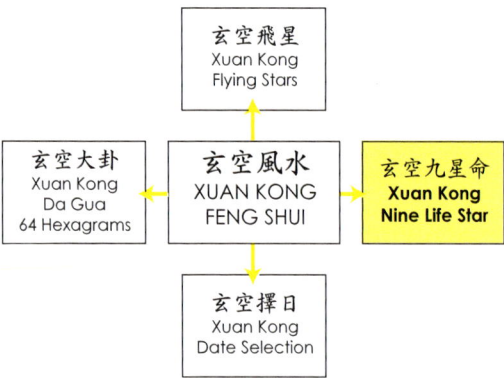

We can use the Xuan Kong Life Star system to help us with a number of practical Feng Shui and interpersonal decisions that make a big impact.

When we assess Feng Shui, we assess four factors: Environment, Buildings, Time and People. This book has been written to complement a number of other Feng Shui titles;

1. *Feng Shui for Homebuyers – Exterior;*
2. *Feng Shui for Homebuyers – Interior;*
3. *Feng Shui for Apartment Buyers;* and
4. *Pure Feng Shui.*

These other books talk about the influence of Environment, Buildings and Time on Feng Shui. This book looks at the final aspect: **People**.

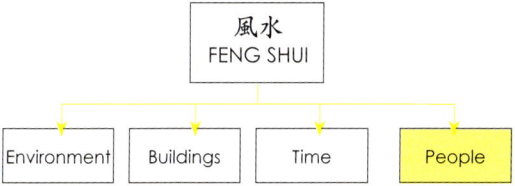

Different people will be affected in different ways by any given environment. The Life Stars directly determine what role the environment plays in the lives of its occupants. Every person is governed by one of the 9 Life Stars. These Stars also help determine key personal characteristics.

In this book, you will learn how the annually changing Xuan Kong Flying Stars interact with your Life Star so that you know what different sectors of your home will bring you. You can then use this information for your own benefit and safety. For maximum benefit, people should seek to align themselves with the direction in their home that yields positive effects. For instance, the #9 Purple Flying Star brings about the potential of career advancement for Star 1 people. Clearly this is a benefit that professionally minded people would like to take advantage of, so they may wish to spend more time absorbing the influence of the #9 Purple Flying Star in their home or place of work. The same Flying Star also indicates a heightened risk of miscarriage for pregnant women though and so pregnant Life Star 1 women should be exercise heightened caution in the presence of this Flying Star, and avoid its influence if possible.

Because the advice generated by this book on Xuan Kong Life Stars takes into account your Life Star when discussing the effects of the Flying Stars, the advice given is highly tailored to your life.

The Positive Side Of You

Your Life Star brings a force to bear on you, wherever you are. This force can have positive or negative effects, depending on the Feng Shui of the environment you reside in.

We are all multi faceted and complex. We have good habits and bad habits; a strong side and a weak side. By correctly tapping into the right Qi your best side will manifest itself more. When you put your best foot forward more in life, more opportunities

and success comes your way. Conversely, if you find yourself under the negative influence of your Life Star, more of your negative personality traits will prevail. Your environment filters out the good or the bad influence of your Life Star. Xuan Kong Feng Shui shows us how we can align ourself to receive the best possible influence. By simply aligning your bed and study desk to correspond with your favourable Personal Directions for example, you can already take one big step towards absorbing the beneficial influence of your Life Star, even whilst you sleep and study! If you are choosing a new home then choosing the correct floor at the correct time will bring further benefits. Avoiding your Personal Grand Duke and Crash Sectors will keep health problems and conflict at bay.

Does all of this mean you must tip-toe around certain rooms in your house or seal them off? No. Feng Shui does not need to become all consuming. If you can easily align your bed so that you receive benefits then why not do so? There are real world limits to what can be done, it is not practical, for instance, to rebuild your home if it does not perfectly cater to the instructions that this book gives. Your ideal floor choice in a condominium may not be available. The list of real world complications goes on.

You can tailor Feng Shui to work for you; making smaller, simple changes so that you reap the maximum possible benefit. The pursuit of good Feng Shui is not intended to take up all of your time and this flexible book is perfect for anyone, no matter how busy or restricted you are in your decisions.

Your Life Star

Everyone falls under the jurisdiction of one of the 9 Life Stars and this will have different consequences for everyone. Your Life Star describes your key skills, characteristics and traits. Some people are creative but reserved, some people are aggressive and driven. What self destructive traits do you have? Do you have a bloated sense of pride or are you prone to gossip? Your Life Star can shine some light on the complexity of your personality and your good and bad traits.

Study of the Life Stars has practical benefits for everyone; it gives you valuable information about others in addition to yourself. Different Life Stars bestow different abilities on people which means that people belonging to each Star will exhibit different characteristics at work. A Star 1 person is diplomatic so they are best suited to roles demanding diplomacy, for example. Accordingly, employers can study the Xuan Kong Life Stars when making work place decisions whilst employees can use the system to help them go about working productively with their colleagues and superiors, even when disagreements arise.

If you become aware of your own harmful tendencies then you can learn to minimize them so you can advance. Similar benefits can be seen in romantic relationships and friendships. Learning that a Star 7 individual needs their space and independence

might help you accommodate this in your dealings with them when you might otherwise have been tempted to be clingy and dependant.

When we understand more about ourselves we can stop ourselves from making mistakes and perhaps forgive certain behaviour in others once we understand where it comes from.

Compatibility Guide

Certain people are, of course, more compatible with each other than others. In partnerships or relationships this takes on a new level of importance. Different Life Stars bestow the qualities of different elements on different people; for example, a Star 1 person has the qualities of water whilst a Star 7 person has the qualities of the Yin Metal element. Just as the elements control, pacify and weaken one another, individuals of the different Stars may dominate, clash with or enrich one another. This book includes a write up of how compatible different Stars are with one another. You may find that a relationship as a Star 1 person with a Star 5 person simply isn't worth the effort. A compatibility guide on each interaction gives you tips on how to best deal with the other Stars for mutual benefit, even taking into account your differences.

Compatible With BaZi Profiling Systems

If you are familiar with the **BaZi Profiling System** then you will be aware that, at first glance, it seems to deal with very similar issues. It can tell us about other preferences and internal view of the world. Do we have an optimistic view of things? Do we blame ourselves too much?

While there is some overlap between the jurisdiction of the Xuan Kong Life Star system and BaZi Profiling System, they are two different systems. They both deal with individual people and their personalities but they are not mutually exclusive. In fact, when studied together, they can be thought of as two pieces of the same puzzle.

The BaZi Profiling System tells us about ourselves and about others. It even tells us things that cannot be observed about others (things people do not communicate). What it can't tell us is how the outside environment plays into the picture. The Xuan Kong Nine Stars help determine *which* qualities are brought out and by what features and external forms in the environment.

Once we know what directions are conducive to good Qi, how external forms (pylons etc) can compound problems related to sectors in the home, which areas of our environment increase the risk of which ailments or even which people can create problems in our lives (compatibility guide) then we can begin shaping our external environment to whatever degree necessary in order to enjoy the most happiness, wealth and success. Xuan

Kong Feng Shui tells you precisely what effect the environment and compass directions will have on which people.

If you are simply interested in learning what makes a person tick rather than making decisions about an ideal environment for them to thrive in then I recommend you take up further study of the BaZi Profiling System. The goal of BaZi is to pinpoint personal deficiencies so that they may be overcome or to highlight personal strengths so that they may be capitalised on.

If you are trying to configure your environment in order to maximize the benefits that your home or place of work bestow upon you in terms of health, wealth and relationships, then the Feng Shui Xuan Kong Life Star system is the one for you.

When you combine the two systems and employ them on yourself you will be able to make the most of your best qualities and then seek out an environment which lets you shine and gives the least resistance. A powerful combination of self improvement and informed decision making!

An Easier Life

Life doesn't have to be difficult. It is possible to effectively dodge conflict, problem situations and health problems if you know they are coming. The Life Stars hold the key to many of the "surprises" that life has in store for us and we can learn to shape our environment to our own advantage. This is exciting stuff! Seeking out the best romantic relationships and business opportunities is a top priority for most people and the power of your Life Star can be called upon in these pursuits.

Even though much is made of the layout of the home with relation to Feng Shui, you won't need to bend over backwards to accommodate the advice given in this book. For instance, where you cannot choose the ideal living floor specified, second and third choices are mentioned. You can take as much or as little from this book as you need without fear of it making you paranoid and prey to "paralysis by analysis". Looking back on your own life, you can most probably think of two or three big mistakes – a bad business deal or choice in romantic partner, perhaps. Avoiding pitfalls of this magnitude in the future is made a whole lot easier when you have some idea of how likely they are to occur. If you can make changes to your environment to further reduce this likelihood then all the better!

I hope that this book expands your world view. Once you know how to utilize them, the Nine Stars can be the harbinger of great fortune instead of misery for you. If you can stay on the 'correct side' of your Star and always position yourself to bask in its positive influence then many happy successes await you.

Joey Yap
July, 2011

 www.facebook.com/joeyyapFB

Author's personal website :
www.joeyyap.com

Academy websites :
www.masteryacademy.com | www.maelearning.com | www.baziprofiling.com

The Yellow Life Star

Life Star 5	Born in
Male	1923, 1932, 1941, 1950, 1959, 1968, 1977, 1986, 1995, 2004
Female	1927, 1936, 1945, 1954, 1963, 1972, 1981, 1990, 1999, 2008

- Please note that the date for the Chinese Solar Year starts on Feb 4. This means that if you were born in Feb 2 of 2002, you belong to the previous year 2001.

Your Xuan Kong Life Star

Your Xuan Kong Life Star is Gua #5, and it is not associated with any trigram. It is instead governed by the Chastity Star (廉貞星).

For the rest of this book, we will refer to your Gua # 5 as Life Star 5.

Basic Attributes of Star 5

Your Life Star 5 is of the Earth element, and as such it takes on some of the qualities of Earth. To visualize the Life Star 5, imagine the vast, flat expanse of the earth and its soil. Your Star lies between all of the others, being of the middle number. Similarly, you occupy the "middle ground" and at your best you tend to be centered, balanced and well rounded.

You are known for your sense of autonomy. You cultivate strength and independence in yourself as you do not like having to rely on anyone else. In this way, you are very much of the earth, which relies on no supporting structure in order to exist , instead helping other things grow and flower! You are usually the kind of person to take control and exert some form of leadership.

You are someone who likes things to follow a set-plan and can thus be very systematic in your approach to the world. Just as each season on earth occupies a period of time, you believe there is a time and place for everything. You dislike the random and the spontaneous. As a Star 5, you possess a determined and resolute character that enables you to stay focused.

Basic Emotions & Temperament

Plus : Independent, strong, self-assertive, persistent, determined

Minus: Egotistic, stubborn, forceful, unadaptive, irritable

五黃　星命
Five Yellow Life Star

28　Xuan Kong Nine Life Star

Directions

Directions

Direction is an integral component of understanding Xuan Kong Nine Life Stars. Different directions in your home and your place of work can either accentuate or depreciate the strength of your Life Star.

Favorable Direction will highlight or enhance the positive traits of your Life Star, while an Unfavorable Direction will diminish or weaken your Life Star and bring out some of its negative attributes.

The Life Star numbers are categorized into two groups: the East Group and the West Group. The names 'East Group' and 'West Group' are just to demarcate the Greater and Lesser Yin transformation of the Tai Ji. They do not literally represent directions.

East Group Life Stars include 1, 3, 4 and 9. Those who are Life Stars 2, 6, 7 and 8 belong to the West Group. The following table will give you a quick reference of the Auspicious and Inauspicious compass directions of the East and West Group.

East Group 東命

卦 Gua	生氣 Shen Qi Life Generating	天醫 Tian Yi Heavenly Doctor	延年 Yan Nian Longevity	伏位 Fu Wei Stability	禍害 Mishaps	五鬼 Five Ghosts	六煞 Six Killings	絕命 Life Threatening
坎 1 Water	東南 South East	東 East	南 South	北 North	西 West	東北 North East	西北 North West	西南 South West
震 3 Wood	南 South	北 North	東南 South East	東 East	西南 South West	西北 North West	東北 North East	西 West
巽 4 Wood	北 North	南 South	東 East	東南 South East	西北 North West	西南 South West	西 West	東北 North East
離 9 Fire	東 East	東南 South East	北 North	南 South	東北 North East	西 West	西南 South West	西北 North West

West Group 西命

	卦 Gua	生氣 Shen Qi Life Generating	天醫 Tian Yi Heavenly Doctor	延年 Yan Nian Longevity	伏位 Fu Wei Stability	禍害 Mishaps	五鬼 Five Ghosts	六煞 Six Killings	絕命 Life Threatening
Male ▶	坤 Kun 2 Earth	東北 North East	西 West	西北 North West	西南 South West	東 East	東南 South East	南 South	北 North
	乾 6 Metal	西 West	東北 North East	西南 South West	西北 North West	東南 South East	東 East	北 North	南 South
	兌 7 Metal	西北 North West	西南 South West	東北 North East	西 West	北 North	南 South	東南 South East	東 East
Female ▶	艮 Gen 8 Earth	西南 South West	西北 North West	西 West	東北 North East	南 South	北 North	東 East	東南 South East

The concepts of Favorable and Unfavorable are derived from the Eight Wandering Stars system of the Ba Zhai Eight Mansion Feng Shui 八宅風水.

Each of the 8 directions is governed by a Star. These Wandering Stars will affect each Xuan Kong Life Star in different ways. Each Life Star has four Favorable Directions governed by Auspicious Stars: Sheng Qi 生氣 (Life Generating), Tian Yi 天醫 (Heavenly Doctor), Yan Nian 延年 (Longevity), and Fu Wei 伏位 (Stability).

The four Unfavorable Directions are governed by Inauspicious Stars and include Huo Hai 禍害 (Mishaps), Wu Gui 五鬼 (Five Ghost), Liu Sha 六煞 (Six Killings) and Jue Ming 絕命 (Life Diminishing).

The following diagram shows you the Favorable and Unfavorable Directions for Star 5. Special note: Star 5 is unique, in that there are different Directions for men and women. As such this section will be divided into Favorable and Unfavorable Directions for Men and for Women.

Taking the Direction using a Compass

You will need a compass – or alternatively, the Joey Yap iLuoPan app for iPhone available at the Apple App Store – to determine the direction of your Main Door, Bed and Stove. Hold your compass or iLuoPan at waist level as shown on the illustration below. Your compass or iLuoPan will align to the magnetic North on its own. All you need to know is how to take your direction as indicated on the following pages.

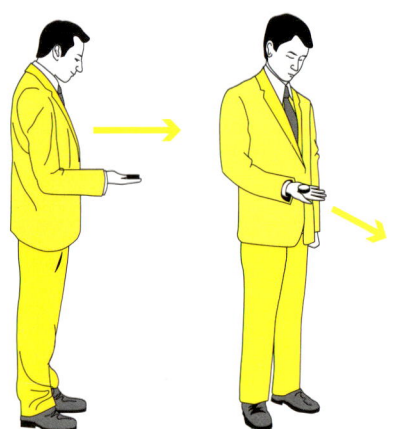

Facing Direction of the Main Door

1. Stand about one foot outside the door looking outwards.

2. Use the square base of your compass to help you align yourself parallel to the door.

3. Read the facing direction on your compass.

Facing Direction of the Bed

1. Measure from the head of the bed where your head is placed when you lie down (the direction the headboard faces) and not the direction your feet face.

Facing Direction of the Stove

1. For modern (gas or electric) stoves, look at the where direction of the cooking knobs (fire igniters) are pointing to determine its facing direction.

2. For traditional stoves that require wood and fire to work, look for their 'fire mouth' as the facing direction.

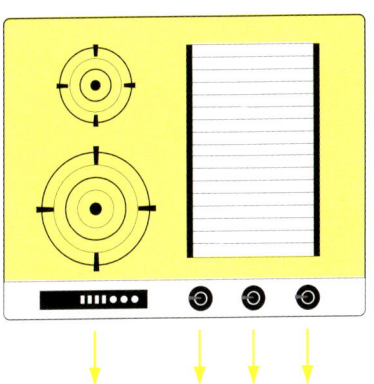

Xuan Kong Nine Life Star

Favorable Directions

Do Take note that if your resultant number is 5, then Males will assume a Life Star 2 and Females will assume Life Star 8.

Men	Women
Northeast 東北 (37.6°-52.5°)	**Southwest** 西南 (217.6°-232.5°)

Life Generating 生氣 (Sheng Qi)

The basic characteristics of the Sheng Qi Star:

It brings about promotions, career advancements, strong money and wealth luck, potential political power and authority, and all-round success.

The Sheng Qi Star represents life-generating Qi or energy. It also represents the Wood Element, and hence, governs the facets of success, authority, nobility, status and wealth in life. Wood relates to growth and advancement in life, and as such is an extremely auspicious Star to tap into.

This Star is suitable for business (commercial), career and wealth-related pursuits. It would therefore be ideal for a business or residence to have its Main Door situated in the Sheng Qi sector as it allows you to tap into these energies to create opportunities for profit and long term wealth opportunities.

Sheng Qi is an active star by nature and thus, it is not conducive for rest or sleep-related activities. It is best to avoid having the bed or bedroom located in this sector or for anyone to sleep facing this direction. Use this sector for your work or for active pursuits instead of relaxing ones.

If this sector is missing from a house or is lacking in the office or the premises of a business, the wealth-related aspects of your career or venture will be considerably weakened and it will be a difficult struggle to amass wealth and prosperity.

Men	Women
West 西 (262.6°-277.5°)	**Northwest** 西北 (307.6°-322.5°)

Heavenly Doctor
天醫 *(Tian Yi)*

The basic characteristics of the Tian Yi Star:

It brings about general good luck and well-being, as well as positive mentor luck or the presence of sound advisors and guidance.

This Star represents the Earth Element and is therefore the determinant of noble people (mentors) and people of caliber and status. It also denotes your health prospects and physical wellbeing. As such, the Tian Yi Star is best utilized to help generate guidance for your career or for any project which you've embarked upon. It will bring about the help and assistance of others.

It is also a useful Star for health purposes, and its benefits can be employed when you need to recuperate, recover, or heal from an illness, surgical procedure or health issue.

When the Tian Yin sector is missing from a home or office, your health is likely to suffer because of it. In addition, you will also find help from noble people hard to come by, especially in times of need in life and career matters. You will come across more obstacles and obstructions which you must overcome on your own without the external help of others.

Since the Tian Yi Star represents nobility, it also governs your reputation, respectability, and your oratory powers. It thus has influence on your powers of speech and persuasion, and has some bearing on how you are perceived by others and how well they respond to your verbal overtures.

Men	Women
Northwest 西北 (307.6°-322.5°)	**West** 西 (262.6°-277.5°)

Life Generating
生氣 *(Sheng Qi)*

The basic characteristics of the Yan Nian Star:

It prolongs and enhances life and improves the quality of your life. It promotes good communication with others which in turn makes for good relationship.

The Yan Nian Star represents the Metal Element, and as such governs speech and the effectiveness of your words. If you are looking to establish good relationships and rapport with others, you will need the help of this Star, since it governs aspects of successful networking, communication and relationship building.

The Yan Nian Star is important for family harmony and domestic bliss. It is also necessary if you wish to build good relationships with co-workers and colleagues. Essentially, it paves the way for smooth interpersonal relations, seldom plagued by misunderstanding, arguments and flare-ups. As such, the presence of the Yan Nian Star is useful for maintaining harmony.

If you are employed in public relations or marketing and you must interact with clients and customers as part of your daily routine, you will find the Qi brought about by this Star very useful to your career.

Do note that if the Yan Nian sector is missing, harmony and unity will be adversely affected, and relations are likely to be tense or strained. At the very least, you can expect more argument and discord with others.

Men	Women
Southwest 西南 (217.6°-232.5°)	**Northeast** 東北 (37.6°-52.5°)

Stability
伏位 *(Fu Wei)*

The basic characteristics of the Fu Wei Star:

It is a Star that promotes calm and keeps you grounded. It allows for peace of mind and rationality. It also promotes good luck.

The Fu Wei Star represents the Wood Element. When qualities or virtues such as calmness and tranquility are required, this is the Star you need! It promotes peace of mind and heightens clarity of thought, so this is also the Star to use if you need to focus, study or make important decisions.

If you wish to practice mediation or undertake religious and spiritual observances, the Fu Wei Star will provide the energies needed for calm and serenity, enhancing mental health and wellbeing.

This Star is most suitably applied to libraries, study areas/zones or other places where concentration is necessary. When considering the home or workplace, this Star can help create areas where the mind can be easily quietened and people can reflect and turn inward.

When the Fu Wei sector is missing from a place, peace of mind will be difficult to attain.

Unfavorable Directions

Do Take note that if your resultant number is 5, then Males will assume a Life Star 2 and Females will assume Life Star 8.

Men	Women
East 東 (82.6°-97.5°)	**South** 南 (172.6°-187.5°)

Mishaps
禍害 *(Huo Hai)*

The basic characteristics of the Huo Hai Star:

It denotes potential calamities, accidents, and mishaps. It undermines good efforts and brings about the risk of mistakes and errors.

The Huo Hai Star represents the Earth Element and is the harbinger of mishaps, loss of wealth, sudden (unfortunate) changes or hassles as well as work-related obstacles. What it does is undermine your efforts and bring about sudden obstructions or problems that will result in a loss of time and energy.

If, for example, the Main Door of a property is located in this direction, you can reasonably expect to encounter quite a few obstacles and problems in your daily life. It is best to work around this area particularly if your main door or office is located in the West sector.

The detrimental effects of a negative star are compounded when it is located within an area that is already affected by negative Feng Shui, so pay attention to the negative structures outside this area.

Men	Women
Southeast 東南 (127.6°-142.5°)	**North** 北 (352.6°-7.5°)

Five Ghosts
五鬼 *(Wu Gui)*

The basic characteristics of the Wu Gui Star:

It brings about betrayal and treachery through back-stabbing, gossip, and rumors. It also denotes endless bickering and fraught tension brought about by arguments.

The Wu Gui Star represents the Fire Element and is the bringer of betrayal, ill-intentioned gossip, rumours, backstabbing, cruelty, petty people and even subterfuge and sabotage. It generally denotes a sense of unease brought upon by less-than-honest speech.

The presence of Wu Gui in a house causes disloyalty and discord amongst family members, affecting relationships and marriages. If it is present in your work place, then you should also watch out for fights and arguments between your colleagues or subordinates and friction or tension with your superiors.

Negative external forms such as (sharp) pylons and jagged rooftops pointing towards a house further aggravate the effects of this Star.

Men	Women
South 南 (172.6°-187.5°)	**East** 東 (82.6°-97.5°)

Six Killings
六煞 (Liu Sha)

The basic characteristics of the Liu Sha Star:

This Star brings about injuries and accidents. It also denotes the possibility of betrayals and dishonesty, and the risk of potential scandals.

The Liu Sha Star relates to the element of Water and is the harbinger of lawsuits and potential scandals. Legal problems at the workplace or adulterous affairs in relation to your marriage or personal relationships could be brought to light.

This Star is also the harbinger of bodily injury, harm and conditions requiring people to undergo physical surgery. Robberies and theft are also likely, and you will have to be careful about what information you share with others and with the general safety of your personal documents and possessions.

Be mindful of the presence of negative external forms, which will compound the adverse effects of this Star. For instance, a Y-shaped road at the Liu Sha sector will result in scandalous affairs, while negative structures as mentioned earlier will compound and exacerbate the harmful effects of the Liu Sha Star.

Men	Women
North 北 (352.6°-7.5°)	**Southeast** 東南 (127.6°-142.5°)

Life Threatening
絕命 *(Jue Ming)*

The basic characteristics of the Jue Ming Star:

It brings about the risk of accidents and major illness, and the threat of miscarriage for pregnant women. It also signals potential for great calamity.

This Star represents the Metal Element and it signifies accidents and illnesses. The energies of the Jue Ming Star are quite severe and so are its adverse effects, bringing with it considerable risk.

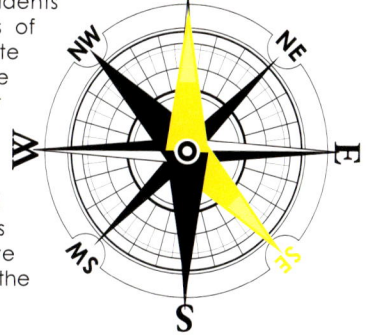

In severe cases, the Jue Ming Star can even cause fatal accidents, ailments or injuries when there are negative external forms outside of the sector.

It is to no surprise that this star is often regarded as the primary star of misfortune and calamity in the study of Ba Zhai Feng Shui. Other than catastrophes and accidents, it can also cause major loss of wealth and theft as well as the cause of breakups or separation in relationships.

Bed Alignment Direction

One of the key Feng Shui factors of the bedroom is how your bed is placed. For starters, your bed should preferably be pushed against a wall, with the headboard also against it. The most important thing you can do when laying out your bedroom with regards to Feng Shui is to make sure your headboard is aligned with your Favorable Direction.

Facing Direction, in the case of bed alignment, refers to the direction of your headboard. This means it is the direction your head faces when you lie down on the bed, and **not** the direction that your feet face.

As a Star 5, your Bed Alignment Directions are:

Male	Female
Northeast	Southwest
West	Northwest
Northwest	West
Southwest	Northeast

Best Floor

A reality of modern life is that most of us do not live in houses these days, instead living in multi story apartments and condominium blocks.

Some of us are pretty mobile and live a nomad-like lifestyle that may require us to stay in high-rise buildings for certain periods of time. As such, it becomes important to select the right floor to reside in. The objective of this is to achieve elemental affinity between you (the occupant) with the energies of a particular floor.

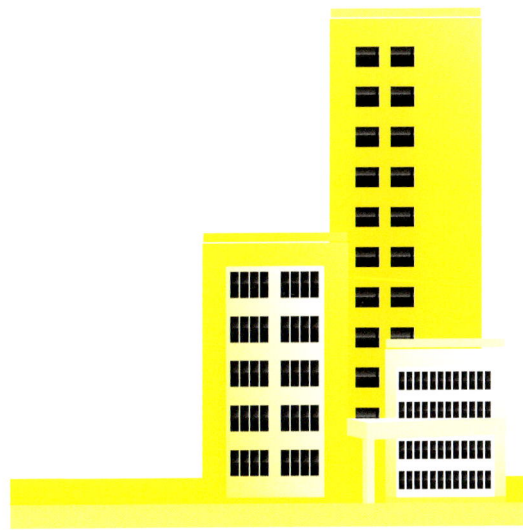

As you are a Star 5 person of the Earth element, the chart below gives you the best floors for you to live on in terms of first choice, second choice, and third choice.

First Choice	Second Choice	Third Choice
5th Floor	2nd Floor	1st Floor
10th Floor	7th Floor	6th Floor
15th Floor	12th Floor	11th Floor
20th Floor	17th Floor	16th Floor
25th Floor	22th Floor	21th Floor
30th Floor	27th Floor	26th Floor
35th Floor	32th Floor	31th Floor
40th Floor	37th Floor	36th Floor
45th Floor	42th Floor	41st Floor
50th Floor	47th Floor	46th Floor

Select :
Fire shaped buildings & Earth shaped buildings

Avoid :
Wood shaped buildings & Metal shaped buildings

Personal Grand Duke Directions

Identifying the Grand Duke Sector is important. Your Personal Grand Duke Sector relates to your birth year. For example, if you are born in the year of the Rat then the Rat is your Personal Grand Duke and we know that the Rat sector is North 2 .

We want to avoid the harmful properties of this area and as you are a Star 5 person, you can locate your Personal Grand Duke Sector in the following directions:

Personal Grand Duke Directions for Male

MALE Birth Year	Personal Grand Duke	Direction
1914, 1950, 1986, 2022	寅 Yin Tiger	東北 3 Northeast 3
1923, 1959, 1995, 2031	亥 Hai Pig	西北 3 Northwest 3
1932, 1968, 2004, 2040	申 Shen Monkey	西南 3 Southwest 3
1941, 1977, 2013, 2049	巳 Si Snake	東南 3 Southeast 3

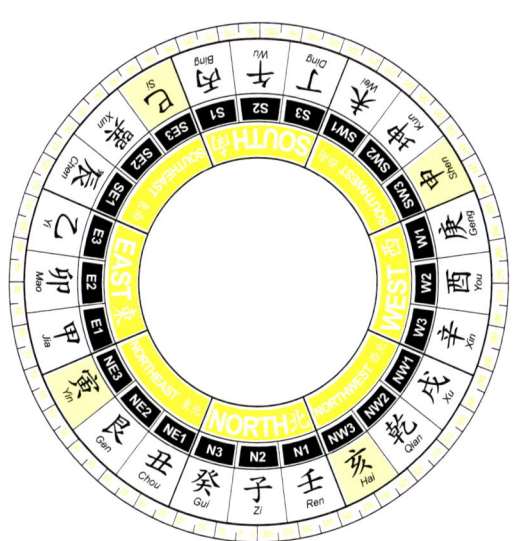

Personal Grand Duke Directions for Female

FEMALE Birth Year	Personal Grand Duke	Direction
1918, 1954, 1990, 2026	午 Wu Horse	南 2 **South 2**
1927, 1963, 1999, 2035	卯 Mao Rabbit	東 2 **East 2**
1936, 1972, 2008, 2044	子 Zi Rat	北 2 **North 2**
1945, 1981, 2017, 2053	酉 You Rooster	西 2 **West 2**

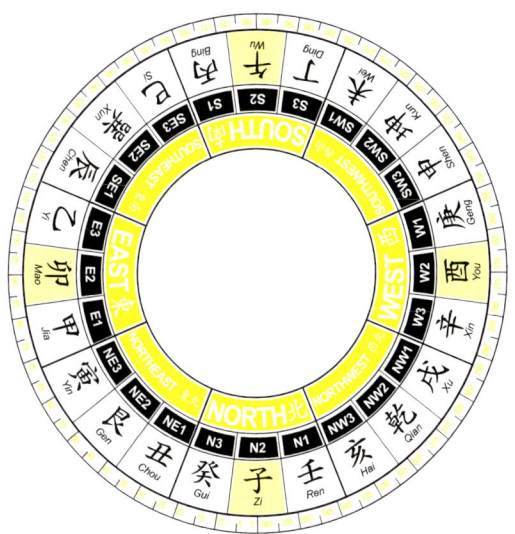

Ideally, you should not have a bathroom or toilet located in these areas of your home above and Sha Qi external features such as pylons, T-junctions, Dead Tree should be avoided. The Sha Qi in the Personal Grand Duke Sector is extremely strong and so all efforts to avoid spending a lot of time in it should be made. It goes without saying that the Personal Grand Duke Sector of your home is not the ideal spot for a bedroom! The Sha Qi in this area of the home is so strong in fact that it is difficult for any further negative Qi to enter!

Personal Clash Directions

Your home will contain Personal Clash Sectors. Spending time in these areas of your home will bring up problems in your life with significant others. As a Star 5 person, you will find your Personal Clash Sectors in the following directions:

Personal Clash Directions for Male

MALE Birth Year	Personal Clash Sector	Direction
1914, 1950, 1986, 2022	申 Shen Monkey	西南 3 Southwest 3
1923, 1959, 1995, 2031	巳 Si Snake	東南 3 Southeast 3
1932, 1968, 2004, 2040	寅 Yin Tiger	東北 3 Northeast 3
1941, 1977, 2013, 2049	亥 Hai Pig	西北 3 Northwest 3

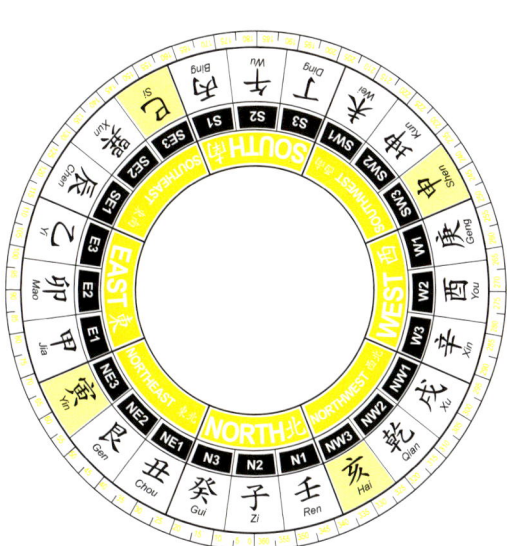

Personal Clash Directions for Female

FEMALE Birth Year	Personal Grand Duke	Direction
1918, 1954, 1990, 2026	子 Zi Rat	北 2 North 2
1927, 1963, 1999, 2035	酉 You Rooster	西 2 West 2
1936, 1972, 2008, 2044	午 Wu Horse	南 2 South 2
1945, 1981, 2017, 2053	卯 Mao Rabbit	東 2 East 2

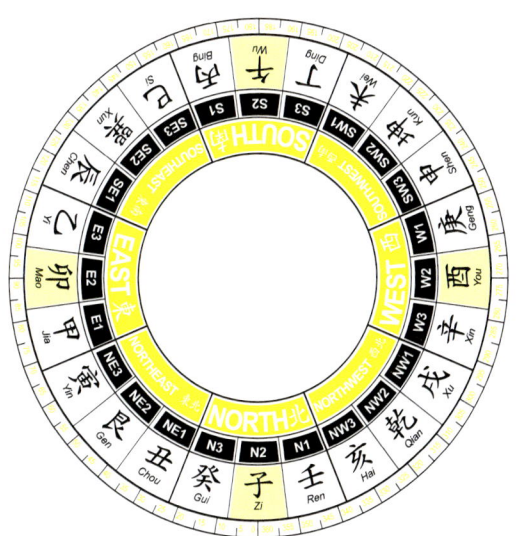

The locations above are a bad place for important features of your home such as the main door, bedroom and kitchen. You should seek to avoid these sectors in the same way you avoid your Personal Grand Duke Sector.

Flying Stars
Effect

Each year, the Xuan Kong Flying Stars fly into a different section of a property, be it your residence or your work space. The effects that these Nine Stars have on you will be different depending on your Life Star. In this section you can find out how different Flying Stars in different sectors will effect you with regards to Feng Shui.

The Flying Stars have both negative and positive attributes, but which facets will show when you see a particular Star, depends on the timeliness and the period.

A few of the Nine Stars are inherently negative, a few are inherently positive in nature and some can be both good and bad. Even then, we must remember that the Stars have the capacity to manifest either their positive or negative facets because in Feng Shui, nothing is ever inherently bad or good forever.

When it comes to Flying Stars, it is important to remember this key principle: Forms activate the Stars and the Stars in turn influence the People. This is what you should keep in mind as you read about the effects of the Nine Stars on your Life Star.

1 ★ → 5 Yellow Life

The effects of the visiting **#1 White Star** on a **5 Yellow Life:**

In terms of Feng Shui effects, the presence of the #1 White Star brings with it negative effects, mainly related to your physical well being. It can can result in quite a few serious situations so pay heed to early warning signs. Some of the problems you're likely to experience include inflammation of the bladder and possible ulcers or problems related to gastritis. Women will have to watch out for any sort of illness involving the reproductive system. A thorough gynecological check-up will be necessary. Furthermore, you may suffer from ear allergies or problems that could lead to something serious, so don't let symptoms persist undetected.

2★ → 5 Yellow Life

The effects of the visiting **#2 Black Star** on a **5 Yellow Life**:

In terms of Feng Shui effects, the presence of the #2 Black can be particularly bad for you in your home. It can instigate loss and some form of depression, and there will also be negative health effects to watch out for. The potential for injury and accidents is increased so don't be reckless. If there are negative features located outside the particular sector where the #2 Black exerts influence, then there is also likely to also be some form of chaos or disruption to your usual way of life. Be prepared for life changing problems.

3★ → 5 Yellow Life

The effects of the visiting **#3 Jade Star** on a **5 Yellow Life**:

In terms of Feng Shui effects, the presence of the #3 Jade can pose a problem for most of the people of Star 5. The energy of the star can manifest in form of serious financial losses, possibly brought about by unscrupulous people. Pay attention to the financial mechanisms of your business if you have one, in order to ensure there is no fraud. You must be alert and attentive as #3 Jade brings about the risk of defecting or betraying employees. At home, you will have to pay attention to the health of the men in the house, particularly of sons who are of Star 5. Chronic or frequent illness with symptoms that persist indicate the need for medical treatment, even if the symptoms seem minor. Finally, in terms of personal finances, keep an eye on your investments as bankruptcy could be around the corner.

4★ → 5 Yellow Life

The effects of the visiting **#4 Green Star** on a **5 Yellow Life:**

In terms of Feng Shui effects, the presence of the #4 Green is likely be the harbinger of poor health and illness. Women in particular have to take note of its arrival as the #4 Green could bring about the possible risk of breast cancer. In general, viral illnesses are likely to be common with the presence of this Star.

The #4 Green also doesn't bode well for Star 5 people who like to take financial risks, as it points towards heavy financial losses. Money may be gambled away or squandered through speculative, high-risk investments that do not pay off.

5★ → 5 Yellow Life

The effects of the visiting **#5 Yellow Star** on a **5 Yellow Life:**

In terms of Feng Shui effects, the presence of the #5 Yellow cannot be taken lightly, with dire consequences for the health of Star 5 people, leading to severe ill health and physical weakening. If there are negative structures outside the area with the presence of Star 5, then some of the risks include physical injuries to the joints and the bones, and in some serious cases, bone cancer. The #5 Yellow also brings about fights and disruptions, so you may find your relationships with those close to you become severely strained. It will be best to take care and proceed carefully. Consider the feelings of others more so than you usually do.

6★ → 5 Yellow Life

The effects of the visiting **#6 White Star** on a **5 Yellow Life:**

In terms of Feng Shui effects, the presence of the #6 White can be quite good for you and your financial growth. This is particularly true if the external features of the relevant sector in your home or work place are positive, thus emphasizing the good effects of the #6 White. Some kind of second income may become feasible. Alternatively, you may enjoy a raise at work or even a windfall from your investments. When there are negative structures outside this sector, however, be prepared for illness and possible health problems. Some of the more serious results of the #6 White include cancer, and for some men of the Star 5 it can result in impotence.

7★ → 5 Yellow Life

The effects of the visiting **#7 Red Star** on a **5 Yellow Life:**

In terms of Feng Shui effects, the presence of the #7 Red can also be good for your financial ventures. The star has many of the same effects #6 White. But again, if there are negative structures outside, it poses some risks to your health. Watch out for food poisoning, allergies, and venereal disease. In terms of interpersonal relations, the #7 Red can cause a heightened sense of tension exacerbated by gossip and backstabbing. On the negative side, this can bring about the fall of some your friendships or relationships, but on the plus side, you will be able to tell apart fair-weather friends from the good ones.

8 ★ → 5 Yellow Life

The effects of the visiting **#8 White Star** on a **5 Yellow Life:**

In terms of Feng Shui effects, the presence of the #8 White is good for money if there are positive features outside this sector, particularly if there are water features.

Some of the negative effects of the #8 White on the Star 5 person are also related to health, particularly with relations to the nose and ears. Furthermore, it can also cause emotional strife and some form of minor or serious depression.

9★ → 5 Yellow Life

The effects of the visiting **#9 Purple Star** on a **5 Yellow Life:**

In terms of Feng Shui effects, the presence of the #9 Purple is quite inauspicious for the Star 5 person, and as such extreme care must be taken. Potential risks in a building include fire hazards. Furthermore, there will also be health problems in the form of eye infections, as well as stomach ulcers.

五黃 星命
Five Yellow Life Star

The Five Elements

The element of your Life Star 5 is Earth, and it is important that you understand the implications of this. In the study of Chinese Metaphysics and Feng Shui, a basic understanding of the Five Elements is integral to success. This section will briefly outline the role of the Five Elements.

The Five Elements are symbolic representations of energy, or Qi. In Feng Shui and in BaZi, the Five Elements are Earth, Metal, Water, Wood, and Fire. Earth represents solidity, stability, and trust, and is associated honour, honesty, and a certain nobility of character.

In order to understand the elements, it's important to understand their relationship to one another. Each element does not exist in isolation. As such, these elements share three important relationships known as 'cycles' that are fundamental to the understanding of Feng Shui: the Productive Cycle, the Controlling Cycle, and the Weakening Cycle.

Productive Cycle

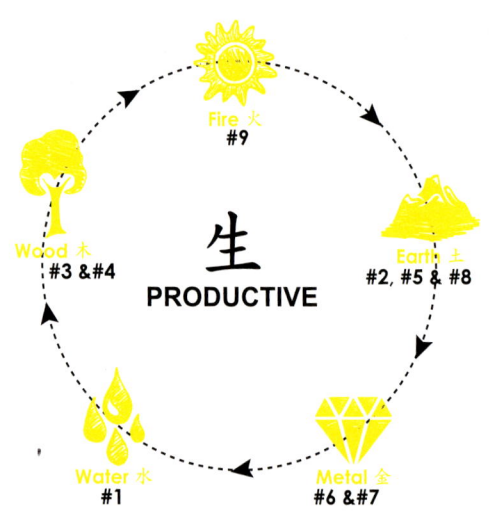

In this cycle,

Water produces Wood
Wood produces Fire
Fire produces Earth
Earth produces Metal
Metal produces Water

This is a cycle where the elements "produce" one another in terms of providing or helping the growth of another. In the case of Water, then, it produces nourishment for trees and plants (i.e. Wood). An element that produces another element means that it strengthens and grows the element that it produces. Here are some simple metaphors might help you visualize this better:

Water waters soil, producing Wood
Wood makes kindling, producing Fire
Fire makes ashes, producing Earth
Earth is mined, producing Metal
Metal melts, producing Water

Controlling Cycle

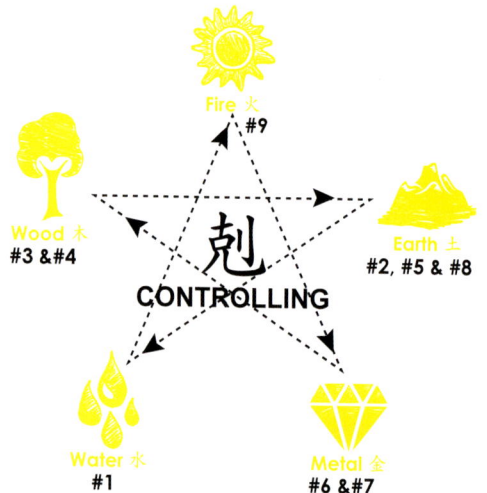

In this cycle,

Fire controls Metal
Metal controls Wood
Wood controls Earth
Earth controls Water
Water controls Fire

This is a cycle where the elements keep each under in "control": an element is countered or subjugated by its controlling element. In this instance, for example, the element of Water controls Fire by putting it out. Here are some simple metaphors to help you visualize it better:

Water extinguishes Fire
Fire melts Metal
Metal cuts Wood
Wood roots tightly grip Earth
Earth contains Water

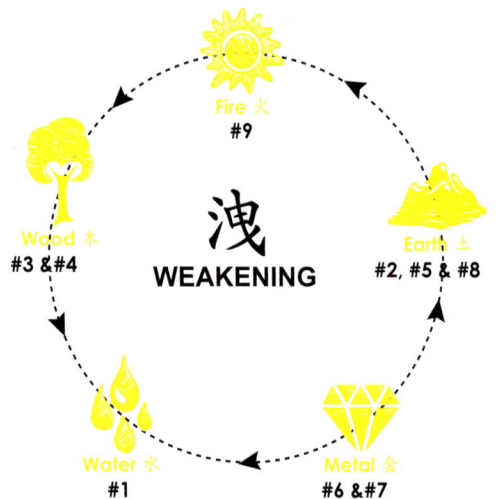

In this cycle,

Water weakens Metal
Metal weakens Earth
Earth weakens Fire
Fire weakens Wood
Wood weakens Water

The Weakening Cycle can be best understood as the reverse of the Productive Cycle, in that the strength of the element is weakened by another in order to keep it in check. Remember, the key to Qi in Feng Shui is balance, and different elements keep other elements from becoming too strong. For example, Wood absorbs Water and therefore weakens it. Again, here are some metaphors for easier visualization:

Water can be partly absorbed by Wood
Wood can be partly burnt by Fire
Fire can be diminished with Earth
Earth is weakened when mined for Metal
Metal is corroded by Water

The following table shows you the Annual Stars for the year 2000 to 2026.

Examine it and figure out where your room lies; in which sector. Take note of the element of that sector and remember that as a Star 5 person, your element is Earth.

2002, 2011, 2020

SE Xun	S Li	SW Kun
6 White	2 Black	4 Green
5 Yellow (E Zhen)	7 Red	9 Purple (W Dui)
1 White	3 Jade	8 White
NE Gen	N Kan	NW Qian

2003, 2012, 2021

SE Xun	S Li	SW Kun
5 Yellow	1 White	3 Jade
4 Green (E Zhen)	6 White	8 White (W Dui)
9 Purple	2 Black	7 Red
NE Gen	N Kan	NW Qian

2004, 2013, 2022

SE Xun	S Li	SW Kun
4 Green	9 Purple	2 Black
3 Jade (E Zhen)	5 Yellow	7 Red (W Dui)
8 White	1 White	6 White
NE Gen	N Kan	NW Qian

2005, 2014, 2023

SE Xun	S Li	SW Kun
3 Jade	8 White	1 White
2 Black (E Zhen)	4 Green	6 White (W Dui)
7 Red	9 Purple	5 Yellow
NE Gen	N Kan	NW Qian

2006, 2015, 2024

SE Xun	S Li	SW Kun
2 Black	7 Red	9 Purple
1 White (E Zhen)	3 Jade	5 Yellow (W Dui)
6 White	8 White	4 Green
NE Gen	N Kan	NW Qian

2007, 2016, 2025

SE Xun	S Li	SW Kun
1 White	6 White	8 White
9 Purple (E Zhen)	2 Black	4 Green (W Dui)
5 Yellow	7 Red	3 Jade
NE Gen	N Kan	NW Qian

2008, 2017, 2026

SE Xun	S Li	SW Kun
9 Purple	5 Yellow	7 Red
8 White (E Zhen)	1 White	3 Jade (W Dui)
4 Green	6 White	2 Black
NE Gen	N Kan	NW Qian

2000, 2009, 2018

SE Xun	S Li	SW Kun
8 White	4 Green	6 White
7 Red (E Zhen)	9 Purple	2 Black (W Dui)
3 Jade	5 Yellow	1 White
NE Gen	N Kan	NW Qian

2001, 2010, 2019

SE Xun	S Li	SW Kun
7 Red	3 Jade	5 Yellow
6 White (E Zhen)	8 White	1 White (W Dui)
2 Black	4 Green	9 Purple
NE Gen	N Kan	NW Qian

These Annual Stars shows you the location of the Stars in a property for the duration of the years specified. Based on the year, the Annual Stars will be located in different sectors of the house. Accordingly, different Annual Stars will affect the Feng Shui of your room in different years.

If the Annual Star of your bedroom is of the same element as your Life Star then the outcome is likely to be prosperous (Productive Cycle). If the Annual Star is your Life Star's controlling element (Controlling Cycle), then the result is likely to be stressful – although this combination is still desirable. But if the Annual Star element is the countering element (Countering Cycle) of your Life Star, then the combination is an unfavorable or inauspicious one for you. (Special note: the #5 Yellow Star is generally an undesirable Annual Star for your bedroom regardless of your Life Star.)

Think about the way the element of the Annual Star and your element (Earth) interact.

Besides the Annual Stars of the year, there also other factors to be considered. These include the Flying Stars chart of your specific house or property with the Sitting and Facing Stars. Advanced students may want to read *Xuan Kong Flying Stars Feng Shui* for further information. These Stars also affect the evaluation of the impact of the Xuan Kong Flying Stars on your property. There are many other ways of assessing the Feng Shui of a property, and it's important to understand that all these factors play an important and related role.

五黄 星命
Five Yellow Life Star

The Good

Authoritative

One of the more significant traits of your Life Star 5 is that you are a very take-charge and be-in-control type of person. You're rarely the type to need instructions from others, and as such you tend to be natural-born leaders. Others take notice of the leadership potential in you and thus defer to your judgment about many things, as you exude the aura of reliability.

Loyal

One thing a Life Star 5 person can rarely be accused of is of being wishy-washy, or fickle. Although you deal with uncertainty like everyone else, you are known for being loyal to people, ideas, and causes that have captured your interest or line up with your principles.

Sensitive

Despite your conservative and strict demeanor, you are actually very compassionate and sensitive on the inside. This means that you can sometimes be thin-skinned and appear take offense easily which surprises others. You always make an effort to empathize with others and help them out. As a Star 5 person, you have a natural aptitude for instinctively knowing who needs your help and you then take them under your wing.

Impartial

Out of all the Life Stars, you are the most suited to being impartial. You take a central, balanced stance on many issues. As such, others often turn to you for unbiased judgment and advice, because your independent state of mind ensures that you try hard to arrive at a conclusion or solution without being overly-influenced by the moods and opinions of others.

壞

The Bad

Headstrong

Because of your reliance on your own skills and plans, you tend to have your own mind made up on many things. This is a good thing, unless it becomes unhealthy, in which the Star 5 person can be one of the most headstrong and stubborn people around, to the point where you absolutely disregard what others have to say if it doesn't fit with your plans or ideas.

Domineering

Your natural leadership skills makes you an instant authority figure in most situations and you are competent in this role while your characteristics are in a healthy, balanced state. But at an unhealthy level, Star 5 people can become domineering individuals. You may be too stubborn to change this habit and you can start to enjoy the feeling of power and domination a little too much.

Indulgent

You tend to pay attention to your own ego a little too frequently which is part of the reason that you are prone to becoming overly dominant and stubborn in the first place! In unhealthy situations you become somewhat self-indulgent and self-absorbed, which gets in the way of your natural inclination towards sensitivity and empathy. You may become aggressive and overly power-hungry in the need to keep your ego satiated and stay on top.

Calculative

Most people tend to make calculated decisions about things to some degree. After all, we have to have some system in place to help us make smart decisions. Yet, you tend to become scheming and cunning to the point of detriment, where you weigh the positives and negatives of all ventures, ideas, and even people against your own plan. This usually happens when you're keen to maintain power or are afraid of losing it.

職業和財富

五黄 星命
Five Yellow Life Star

• Leadership

You tend to be very much at the head of things where work is concerned, and this is particularly true if you're in entrepreneurship or in business. You make decisions soundly and swiftly, and are thus seen as an asset by both colleagues and superiors, while subordinates often feel like they can rely on you. You tend to know how to direct others in a scenario to get the best results.

• Organized

You tend to enjoy structure and arrangement, and deplore last-minute impulsiveness; after all, it leaves no time for backup arrangements to be made. As such, you tend to be quite meticulous about the things you have to do, and most work projects that fall under your helm benefit from your careful attention to detail. Others tend to consider this an invaluable trait and often seek your help in implementation.

• Independent

A crucial Star 5 characteristic that you display in the workplace is the ability to get things done without external influence. In other words, you tend to be proactive and forge your own path

in getting your tasks done. You prefer to be in the driver's seat, and it does not really bother you if others don't come along for the ride. This is good in the sense that you don't feel the need to wait for others before getting started, but it's also important to make sure you don't isolate yourself too much from collaboration and teamwork.

• Conservative

You can be straight-laced in your approach to your job role and tasks. This is not necessarily a bad thing, but sometimes it's necessary to break free of the rules once you understand why they're there. A sense of rebelliousness once in awhile can also be a boon to your creativity.

Suitable Job Roles

- **Real estate agent, property dealer and investor**

As an Earth element, Star 5 people will do well in fields related to the Earth, and real estate and property is one which will bring you quite a bit of wealth luck. Your strong appetite for knowledge also makes you an informed agent or investor, which is the kind of quality that enables your clients to build long-term trust in you.

- ## Government or civil servant

Star 5 people tend to do well in a bureaucratic system, as the rules and traditions don't bother you. In fact, you thrive when working within a well-organised system, and find ways within the bounds of these systems to be incredibly productive and far-reaching in your goals and endeavors. As such, government or civil service work may be extremely-suited to your strengths.

- ## Educator, teacher

You will thrive as a teacher, educators, trainer or coaching leaders. This is because your sense of authority and confidence makes you a natural head of affairs and others feel safe under

your tutelage. Furthermore, you are determined and you do not give up on your students easily. You are considerate and have a genuine concern for the welfare, well being and success of the people under your wing.

• Businessperson, entrepreneur

The business ventures or entrepreneurship you will likely do well in are again the industries related to the element of Earth. These include agriculture, animal husbandry, and even trading. Your sharp sense of business acumen and no-nonsense individuality enables you to make firm, fast decisions. Your commitment to playing by the rules ensures that you do not take too many potentially loss-making decisions.

Career and Wealth Guide

• Be less controlling

While independence and authority is a good thing, you must guard against letting this all-consuming need for power dominate you! In the modern workplace, this is always a sneaky temptation, and Star 5 people, because of your strong personalities, may be prone to becoming domineering to the point where you start isolating or antagonizing others. It will benefit you in the long run if you fight against these tendencies.

• It's okay to be playful

Your adherence to structure and organization is exemplary, and it's often what keeps the ship afloat during many of your work projects and career moves. With that said, you need to strive to incorporate some play in your routine, as well. Once in awhile, remind yourself to loosen up and forget about the rules and let the chips fall where they may. The results will prove to be interesting!

- ## Cultivate networks

Your sense of autonomy in how you approach your work is your strength, but other must still be included in your efforts if you hope to succeed in the modern workplace. Whether or not you work alone, it is important that you build strong networks. This means that you will have to make an effort to reach out to others – your aura of power can be imposing and inscrutable to others, who may be intimidated.

• Continue learning

Knowledge is important to you, and it pays well to always keep your mind refreshed by learning new things related to your career, or to your financial ventures. Your pride may sometimes stop you from asking questions, so even things out by doing your own research, particular in matters of finance where knowledge mitigates risk. You are a "collector", of skills, information, and talents. Continue to cultivate this quality.

• Incorporate flexibility

Not everything has to go the way you planned, particularly if you are launching a project with others. Similarly, sometimes financial ventures or investments in stocks or shares requires some modification on a day to day basis. You must learn to adapt to the exigencies of a situation, instead of insisting of staying a particular course because it was part of your initial plans.

Famous Personalities :

Richard Branson,
Lakshmi Mittal,
Oprah Winfrey,
Jerry Yang

人際關係

五黄 星命
Five Yellow Life Star

Guide for Relationships

As a Star 5 person, you present an enigma to others – but an attractive one. With your commanding presence and sense of confidence, you will soon learn that others are quite naturally drawn to you. Most importantly, you can give off a very good first impression, and this is something you should be able to capitalize on and use to the best of your ability!

After familiarizing themselves with the strong character your project, other people don't expect shyness and tentativeness from you in matters of love and romance. But this is true – you possess a tantalizing mix of strength and vulnerability. Don't be afraid to show this side of you; you will win over some long-lasting adoration and attention if you are willing to reveal your 'softer' side. Your self confidence means that you often make decisions on your own and state your opinions in a frank manner, and this can be rather intimidating to your partner or object of interest. Sharing your vulnerabilities is an invitation that may bring your partner closer to your life, and is a welcome sign that you are capable of rewarding intimacy.

However, when you meet someone who you really like, you can take the initiative and sometimes become quite aggressive. In terms of romance, you need to remember that the other person is not there to be 'won', and that you should instead feel out the situation and proceed according to how the other person responds. Do not try and "bully" them into reacting positively.

In long term relationships or marriage, you tend to do quite well. This is because when you pick someone to share your future with, you do so after after thinking long and hard. When you do choose someone, you choose someone with the intention of staying with them for life. Most Star 5 people are the sort of people who stay married happily without ever succumbing to the the need to 'search' for others or seek a change. If you put your mind to it and remember to share your softer side with your spouse, you will be able to create a family and a life that will do you proud.

Star 5 in relationships:

Star 5 people have a strongly possessive nature and are usually dedicated partners. They often shift back and forth between passion and coolness.

健康

五黄 星命
Five Yellow Life Star

Health

Body parts and organs that are related to Star 5: Liver, spleen and lungs.

Your Star 5 represents the liver and the stomach and related digestive systems, as well as the lungs. One of the key weaknesses of a Star 5 person is food, and particularly certain types of food – you have a sweet tooth and you enjoy spicy food. As such, you are likely to have stomach problems or issues with digestion if you over-indulge, which you sometimes have a tendency of doing. Watch out for gastritis, gastric ulcers, irritable bowel syndrome, and frequent bouts of stomach flu.

Any long-term health plan you create will be need to be one where you make significant alterations to your diet. This does not mean that you have to deprive yourself of sweet or spicy food entirely, but it does mean that you have to consume them in moderation.

Some related illnesses that can be quite serious for you include gastric or colon cancer, and so thorough scans and regular check-ups will be necessary.

Your skin is also a sensitive region that can frequently be afflicted with allergies and rash, so be sure to consume the proper nutrients and see a dermatologist for a long-term cure if a particular problem crops up with frequency. As you get older, sore muscles and back, chest, and feet can also present you with recurring problems and discomfort. You may want to focus on strength-enhancing exercise like yoga or Pilates that will help you build muscle tone and force.

Potential health concerns:

Poor overall health

Recurring or chronic health problems

Susceptibility to the common cold or flu

Internal bleeding or injury

Insomnia

The tendency to feel worried, anxious or depressed

五黄　星命
Five Yellow Life Star

This section examines your compatibility as a Star 5 with other people who have the same and different Stars. No person goes through life completely alone. Relationships with others form the bedrock of good career networking. Friendships and relations with loved ones, spouses, partners and family make everything worth while. It is necessary to understand how compatible people with different Stars are to prevent conflict and missed opportunities. Bear in mind that issues of compatibility are not definite or set in stone. There are exceptions to every rule. In addition, **the quality of Feng Shui** in your environment helps dictate whether positive or negative traits in people manifest themselves and thus it weighs in on the quality of your relationships with those people. This section serves as a good guide on your relationships with other people of different Stars.

At a glance, Star 5 people have strong personalities and are therefore susceptible to being misunderstood by others. Most tend to see you as someone intimidating or beyond their league, while some others tend to find you forceful. This is not to say that all your relations with others are necessarily doomed, but that you are unique and an acquired

taste, and as such you should be prepared to put in some work to make your social and professional connections succeed.

Because you are an Earth Star, you will have good relations with people of Stars 2 and 8 because both of those are also Earth Stars. There is likely to be sincerity and honesty in your dealings, especially in terms of professional relations and partnerships. Your relations with Star 1 will also benefit you, because Star 1 is of the Water element and the Earth element counters Water.

You will have to be cautious with people of Stars 3 and 4, as those Stars are of the Wood element and as you will remember, Wood counters the Earth element. You will have to proceed carefully and be cautious, as there can be potential loss for you if you're not careful. Your interaction with a fellow Star 5 person is likely to be as sweet as honey if it goes as well, or absolutely bitter if both of you end up not liking each other!

The chart below lists element people or sectors you can utilise to improve your compatibility with other Star people.

	Compatibility with others Stars (Individuals)	Seek help from this element people or use this sector
Star 5	Stars 2, 5 & 8 (Earth Element)	Earth
	Stars 3 & 4 (wood Element)	Fire
	Stars 6 & 7 (Metal Element)	Water
	Star 9 (Fire Element)	Wood
	Star 1 (Water Element)	Metal

巽 SE Xun	離 S Li	坤 SW Kun
4 Green WOOD	**9** Purple FIRE	**2** Black EARTH
3 Jade WOOD	**5** Yellow EARTH	**7** Red METAL
8 White EARTH	**1** White WATER	**6** White METAL
艮 NE Gen	坎 N Kan	乾 NW Qian

The following pages will explain in detail the compatibility factor of a Star 5 person with people of all other nine Stars through the Compatibility Meter. The Compatibility Guides give you tips for managing the relationships in question.

| **5** Yellow | compatibility with | **1** White |

Compatibility Meter

When a Star 5 person comes together with a Star 1 person, the result is likely to be harmonious and beneficial for you in particular. Star 1 individuals, being of the Water element, "go with the flow". This means that they are likely to conform to your wishes and commanding behavior without conflict. This is ideal in some business situations and plays into your need to be in the driving seat. You can utilize their creative talents and brilliant way of thinking in your own plans. They share your love of autonomy and independence and that means they are unlikely to weigh you down or become dependent. On a personal level, you may be able to confide the most in Star 1 people on the rare occasion that you need to do so as they are known to be excellent listeners. They are not quick to judge and may be highly tolerant

of your candid approach which others may write off as rudeness. In addition, you may see them as suitable romantically because they will allow you to retain your independence.

Compatibility Guide

You must be aware of your calculative tendencies. It may be too tempting for you to simply "use" a Star 1 individual without giving thought to their needs and interests. This will not be beneficial to you in the long run and once they catch on to this fact you are likely to lose their support. You work best when pursuing a common goal and helping each other to that effect so try and align yourself in the same direction for the most beneficial partnership. Romantically, you might have to make an effort to kick back and have more fun with them because they do enjoy being active. You may have to learn to embrace their spontaneous approach to some situations.

| 5 Yellow | compatibility with | 2 Black |

Compatibility Meter

When a Star 5 person comes together with a Star 2 person, the result is likely to be good, especially for you. Star 2 individuals do not share your all consuming thirst for power and this means you are unlikely to lock horns when you meet. Star 2 individuals, possessing tact and social skills that you do not, can make for strong ally, opening doors for you in your career. When you delegate a task you can trust that it will be completed to a satisfactory level. You may sometimes, however, need to push them a little bit as they can become stagnant and lazy if left to their own devices. The inner "coach" in you may take some pleasure in knowing that being around you might help them learn to become more assertive themselves. On a personal level, you will find them caring and

forgiving – they may be more likely to tolerate your unique personality than people of other Stars which makes them suitable candidates for friendship. Romantically, however, they can become dependent and clingy, suffocating your sense of autonomy. They may lose themselves in the face of your forceful and dominating personality and simply come to mirror your point of view.

Compatibility Guide

In order to make this a friendship or romantic relationship work, you need to be aware that things can become unbalanced if left unchecked. It will be important to be humble with the Star 2 person, as allowing your ego to become uncontrollable will prove unattractive to a Star 2 person. You find being in charge pleasurable but it is never healthy to have too much dominance in relationship and passive Star 2 individuals will do little to stop this from happening. Encourage Star 2 individuals to stand up for themselves and retain their independence to prevent issue.

| **5** Yellow | compatibility with | **3** Jade |

Compatibility Meter

When you and a Star 3 person get together, the potential for a power struggle exists. Like you, they don't mince their words and say exactly what they mean; a rare trait you admire. Unfortunately, when two straight talking people get together, explosive results can be ensue when a difference of opinion exists! Star 3 individuals work best when they are allowed to do things on their own terms. You have your own ideas about how things should be done, however, which can lead to friction and conflict. This is made worse by the intense nature of Star 3 people. You might do well to curtail your conflict encouraging behavior, however, because when you get Star 3 people on your side you will find that they can be helpful and generous. Romantically speaking, Star 3 individuals fall hard and fall fast. They

can develop feelings for you which you may be unable or unwilling to reciprocate. For their sake you must be careful not to lead them astray and pursuing a relationship with them may not be wise.

Compatibility Guide

In general, this is a good combination, but you need to be careful that the Star 3 doesn't weaken you or deplete your energy in the long run. The prerequisite is that both of you reach a consensus on certain key issues, particularly if this is a relationship that is meant to be professional. Do not allow pride get in the way of a proper assessment. Exercise caution before becoming involved romantically.

| **5** Yellow | compatibility with | **4** White |

Compatibility Meter

When you and a Star 4 person get together, the outcome for you may be undesirable. This is likely because Star 4 is a Wood Element, and as such can control your Earth element. You may find that they are able to charm you into doing their bidding, being of surprisingly strong mind despite their gentle exterior. You might not be able to form an efficient business partnership with Star 4 individuals as they are impractical and not well suited to getting things done. On a personal level, friendships are also unlikely to flourish; this is because of their tendency to keep others at a distance. You can become suspicious of this behavior as you find it hard to understand. A romance with a Star 4 individual will rarely to be fruitful. They value the mystery, drama and ever changing dynamic of an exciting relationship. Your direct approach and

dislike on relying on others means that the kind of warm, caring relationship a Star 4 individual may seek with you is not forthcoming. In a negative state of mind, Star 4 people can come to be dependent and clingy which does not sit well with your independence and need to feel free.

Compatibility Guide

To understand your relations with the Star 4 person, you must understand that there is a likelihood that the Star 4 person may use certain psychological tricks to trip you up. This is done not so much out of spite or meanness, but simply to gain the upper hand. You need to continue to approach them in a sincere and honest way to see if the relationship is worth pursuing, particularly if this is a romance or a potential friendship. Mutual suspicion on both sides will leave both parties playing guessing games, which is damaging in the long run.

| **5** Yellow | compatibility with | **5** Yellow |

Compatibility Meter

When you and a Star 5 person get together, the outcome may well be prosperous for you both. Obviously, being of the same Star means that you share the same stronger qualities. Whether or not this creates a problem depends entirely upon your opinions. If your both have the same opinion about something then you will find validation in each other. If you disagree, however, then watch out! At the workplace you will find yourself competing directly with other Star 5 individuals but this is by no means a bad thing – competition encourages growth, after all. Mutual respect will ensue and this can form the bedrock of a great friendship. It is worth noting that because there is strong basic affinity and mutual attraction between Star 5 people, conflict and arguments are likely to be short lived and easily put in the past.

Compatibility Guide

If it's a business partnership or romantic relationship that you have with another Star 5 person, you'll have to be rational in evaluating the others qualities. However, if both Star 5 people are constantly at odds with each other, then the relationship is likely to go badly. You will both need to become aware of your controlling nature and some give and take will be the order of the day. It will be best to terminate the relationship early and cut your losses instead of staying on in what could be damaging or cause crises. This is because when relationships between two Star 5 people go bad, they tend to go very bad with a lot of acrimony on both sides.

| **5** Yellow | compatibility with | **6** White |

Compatibility Meter

When you and a Star 6 person get together, your interactions may not go smoothly. You like things out in the open and you don't like a lack of straight forward communication in others. Star 6 individuals are prone to being distant. They lead a highly principled life and this means that to a certain degree they wall themselves off from others. The more forceful you are in the trying to get them to open up, the worse this problem will become. Because of this, you probably won't be able to immediately hit it off as friends or lovers. Star 6 individuals work best in positions which let them arbitrate and delegate. This means that they may not have any place in your plans which usually call for people who can work according to your plan. When a Star 6 individual is your superior,

however, you may well find that you agree on what course of action needs to be taken – your by the book approach may align perfectly with their rule abiding plans.

Compatibility Guide

You will have to persevere if you wish you get to know the Star 6 person, which essentially means you'll have to put your ego aside which will present you with some difficulty. If you can learn to show some restraint in your approach and let the caring side you possess deep down show then a Star 6 person may slowly reveal themselves to you. They can prove to be very lively, generous, and benevolent people. If you're similarly guarded, then the potential for a long-term union looks dim, particularly if you're concealing ulterior motives from the Star 6 person.

| **5** Yellow | compatibility with | **7** Red |

Compatibility Meter

When you and a Star 7 person come together, you probably won't see eye to eye at first. Star 7 individuals have a thirst for life: they enjoy luxury and vivacious living. They are bubbly and highly sociable and like to just have a good time. You barely even know what fun is because you are always so wrapped up in your plans! At work, this personality may be less appropriate and they can seem to be more concerned with themselves than with deadlines or teamwork. Entering into a relationship with a Star 7 individual, however may prove to be a great exercise in personal development for you. Let them show you what it means to let your hair down and live a little because it is unlikely you will allow yourself to do is if left to your own devices. Whether or

not a romantic relationship can work in the long term is uncertain. This is because Star 7 people need attention and you are not prone to indulging this need in others. You are used to being in charge and when you have to start pandering to someone elses constant need for attention you feel that this weakens you.

Compatibility Guide

You may be wise to avoid entering into business partnerships or work situations with Star 7 people but socially and romantically you may benefit from them in the short term or at a certain casual distance. Although a deep connection may be out of the question this may be alright with you because you do not necessarily need one, preferring to rely mainly on yourself.

| **5** Yellow | compatibility with | **8** White |

Compatibility Meter

When you and a Star 8 person come together, the outcome is likely to be very good. Star 8 individuals are not weak minded but they also avoid arguments. This can sit well with you and this trait facilitates your need to be the boss! Out and out conflict will seldom arise. In the work place, Star 8 individuals have a work style which you like. They are cautious and reliable and you will have no problem getting them to stick to any rules you lay down. Their optimism gives them a "can do" attitude which helps them get things done, albeit, slowly. Others might say that they may make for dull friends because they are fairly inexpressive but you see this as a good thing – when left to decide, you choose less exciting friends anyway. Romantically, you might become frustrated at their inability to articulate their true feelings.

If you hurt their feelings, which can easily happen when you get aggressive or speak without considering the effect of your words, resentment will likely begin to grow within them. They will continue to project a cool demeanor until something snaps.

Compatibility Guide

There must not be any suspicion on behalf of either party, particularly on your end, or you will start becoming calculative in order to gain the upper hand, and this will not end well. The best thing you can do to avoid the other person becoming increasingly disillusioned with you and reaching breaking point is to be mindful of the way you deal with them. When someone does not visibly show offense or vocally object you can mistakenly believe that no damage was done.

| 5 Yellow | compatibility with | 9 Purple |

Compatibility Meter

When you and a Star 9 person come together, the results are likely to be beneficial. You will find that you can nurture a Star 9 person, taking the form of a mentor or coach of sorts. You will find that you have a lot to learn from each other, and you tend to share similar goals and ideas on how things should be done. A personal relationship or a friendship might be inadvisable however, as you may end up hurting the Star 9 person with your emotion driven behavior.

Compatibility Guide

To make partnership with a Star 9 person work, you need to have strength of your own and not expect the Star 9 person to do things for you – which typically will not be a problem for you, since you loathe giving up your independence easily. But be sure you don't slide into a pattern of relying too much on the Star 9 person to pick up the slack, because they are prone to doing so and if you let them carry extra weight too often they can begin to feel unhappy. In a more personal relationship like a friendship or a romance, you should steer clear also of antagonizing the Star 9 person by being too forceful. Give Star 9 person ample space, or else you will only push them away.

About Joey Yap

Joey Yap first began learning about Chinese Metaphysics from masters in the field when he was fifteen.

Despite having graduated with a Commerce degree in Accounting, Joey never became an accountant. Instead, he began to give seminars, talks and professional Chinese Metaphysic consultations in Malaysia, Singapore, India, Australia, Canada, England, Germany and the United States, becoming a household name in the field.

By the age of twenty-six, Joey became a self-made millionaire and in 2008, he was listed in The Malaysian Tatler as the Top 300 Most Influential People in Malaysia and Prestige's Top 40 Under 40.

His practical and result-driven take on Feng Shui and BaZi sets him apart from other older, traditional masters and practitioners in the field. He shows people how the ancient teachings can be utilized for tangible REAL world benefits. The success he and his clients enjoy, thanks to his advice, is positive proof that Feng Shui and BaZi Astrology works, whether everyone believes in it or not!

Today, Joey has helped and worked with governments and the wealthiest people in Singapore, Hong Kong, China, Malaysia and Japan. His clients include multinationals, developers, tycoons and royalties. On Bloomberg, he is featured on-air as a regular guest on the subject of Feng Shui annual forecasts. He is retained by twenty-five top Malaysian property developers to help determine suitable candidates to take top management, change their space and Feng Shui mechanism, the way they make decisions, and understand the natural cosmic energies that can influence their decision-making.

Every year he conducts his 'Feng Shui and Astrology' seminar to a crowd of more than 3500 people at the Kuala Lumpur Convention Center. He also takes this annual seminar on a world tour to Frankfurt, San Francisco, New York, Las Vegas, Toronto, Sydney and Singapore.

The Joey Yap Consulting Group is the world's largest and first specialized metaphysics consultation firm. His consultancy, and professional speaking and training engagements with Microsoft, HP, Bloomberg, Citibank, HSBC and many more have seen the benefits of Classical Feng Shui and BaZi find their way into corporate environment and culture. Celebrities, property developers and other large organizations turn to Joey when they need the best.

After years of field-testing and fine-tuning his teachings, he has put together a team in the form of Joey Yap Research International. The objective of this Research Team is to scientifically track and verify the positive impact of Feng Shui and BaZi on subjects and ultimately to assist more people in achieving their life goals.

The Mastery Academy of Chinese Metaphysics which Joey founded teaches thousands of students from all around the world about Classical Feng Shui, Chinese Astrology and Face Reading. Many graduates have gone on to become successful in their own right, becoming sought after consultants, setting up their own consultancy businesses or even becoming educators, passing on Chinese Metaphysics knowledge to others.

Joey has also created the Decision Referential Technology™, offering decision reformation training on how to make better decisions in business and in personal life. He has led his team of highly trained consultants to help clients create more positive change in corporate boardrooms and increase production in their companies, helping people see their business outlook for each year so they may anticipate, plan and execute their strategies successfully.

Joey's work has been featured regularly in various popular global publications and networks like Time, Forbes, the International Herald Tribune and Bloomberg. He has also written columns for The New Straits Times, The Star and The Edge – Malaysia's leading newspapers. He has achieved bestselling author status with over sixty-five books, which have sold more than three million copies to-date.

His success is not limited to matters of Feng Shui and BaZi. Although his success is a product of them, he is also a successful entrepreneur, leading his own companies and property investment portfolio. When not teaching metaphysics or consulting around the world, Joey is a Naruto-fan, avid snowboarder and is crazy for fruits de mer.

Author's personal website :

 www.joeyyap.com

Joey Yap on Facebook:

 www.facebook.com/JoeyYapFB

MASTERY ACADEMY
OF CHINESE METAPHYSICS
Your **Preferred** Choice to the Art & Science of Classical Chinese Metaphysics Studies

Bringing **innovative** techniques and **creative** teaching methods to an ancient study.

Mastery Academy of Chinese Metaphysics was established by Joey Yap to play the role of disseminating this Eastern knowledge to the modern world with the belief that this valuable knowledge should be accessible to anyone, anywhere.

Its goal is to enrich people's lives through accurate, professional teaching and practice of Chinese Metaphysics knowledge globally. It is the first academic institution of its kind in the world to adopt the tradition of Western institutions of higher learning - where students are encourage to explore, question and challenge themselves and to respect different fields and branches of study - with the appreciation and respect of classical ideas and applications that have stood the test of time.

The art and science of Chinese Metaphysics studies – be it Feng Shui, BaZi (Astrology), Mian Xiang (Face Reading), ZeRi (Date Selection) or Yi Jing – is no longer a field shrouded with mystery and superstition. In light of new technology, fresher interpretations and innovative methods as well as modern teaching tools like the Internet, interactive learning, e-learning and distance learning, anyone from virtually any corner of the globe, who is keen to master these disciplines can do so with ease and confidence under the guidance and support of the Academy.

It has indeed proven to be a center of educational excellence for thousands of students from over thirty countries across the world; many of whom have moved on to practice classical Chinese Metaphysics professionally in their home countries.

At the Academy, we believe in enriching people's lives by empowering their destinies through the disciplines of Chinese Metaphysics. Learning is not an option - it's a way of life!

MASTERY ACADEMY
OF CHINESE METAPHYSICS™

MALAYSIA
19-3, The Boulevard, Mid Valley City, 59200 Kuala Lumpur, Malaysia
Tel : +603-2284 8080 | Fax : +603-2284 1218
Email   : info@masteryacademy.com
Website : www.masteryacademy.com

Australia, Austria, Canada, China, Croatia, Cyprus, Czech Republic, Denmark, France, Germany, Greece, Hungary, India, Italy, Kazakhstan, Malaysia, Netherlands (Holland), New Zealand, Philippines, Poland, Russian Federation, Singapore, Slovenia, South Africa, Switzerland, Turkey, U.S.A., Ukraine, United Kingdom

www.masteryacademy.com | +603 - 2284 8080

Mastery Academy around the world

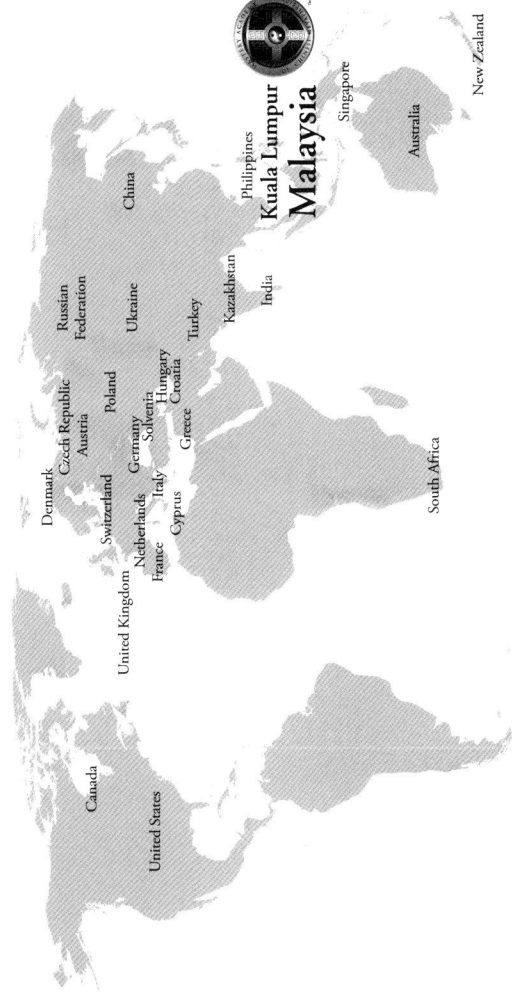

www.masteryacademy.com | +603 - 2284 8080

JOEY YAP CONSULTING GROUP

Pioneering Metaphysics - Centric Personal Coaching and Corporate Consulting

The Joey Yap Consulting Group is the world's first specialised metaphysics consultation firm. Founded in 2002 by renown international Feng Shui and BaZi consultant, author and trainer Joey Yap, the Joey Yap Consulting Group is a pioneer in the provision of metaphysics-driven coaching and consultation services for individuals and corporations.

The Group's core consultation practice areas are Feng Shui and BaZi, which are complimented by ancillary services like Date Selection, Face Reading and Yi Jing Divination. The Group's team of highly-trained professional consultants are led by Principal Consultant Joey Yap. The Joey Yap Consulting Group is the firm of choice for corporate captains, entrepreneurs, celebrities and property developers when it comes to Feng Shui and BaZi-related advisory and knowledge.

Across Industries: Our Portfolio of Clients

Our diverse portfolio of both corporate and individual clients from all around the world bears testimony to our experience and capabilities.

Joey Yap Consulting Group is the firm of choice for many of Asia's leading multi-national corporations, listed entities, conglomerates and top-tier property developers when it comes to Feng Shui and corporate BaZi.

Our services also engaged by professionals, prominent business personalities, celebrities, high-profile politicians and people from all walks of life.

JOEY YAP CONSULTING GROUP

Name (Mr./Mrs./Ms.): _____

Contact Details

Tel: _____ Fax: _____

Mobile : _____

E-mail: _____

What Type of Consultation Are You Interested In?
☐ Feng Shui ☐ BaZi ☐ Date Selection ☐ Corporate Events

Please tick if applicable:
☐ Are you a Property Developer looking to engage Joey Yap Consulting Group?

☐ Are you a Property Investor looking for tailor-made packages to suit your investment requirements?

Please attach your name card here.

Thank you for completing this form. Please fax it back to us at:

Malaysia & the rest of the world
Fax : +603-2284 2213   Tel : +603-2284 1213

www.joeyyap.com

Feng Shui Consultations

For Residential Properties
- Initial Land/Property Assessment
- Residential Feng Shui Consultations
- Residential Land Selection
- End-to-End Residential Consultation

For Commercial Properties
- Initial Land/Property Assessment
- Commercial Feng Shui Consultations
- Commercial Land Selection
- End-to-End Commercial Consultation

For Property Developers
- End-to-End Consultation
- Post-Consultation Advisory Services
- Panel Feng Shui Consultant

For Property Investors
- Your Personal Feng Shui Consultant
- Tailor-Made Packages

For Memorial Parks & Burial Sites
- Yin House Feng Shui

BaZi Consultations

Personal Destiny Analysis
- Personal Destiny Analysis for Individuals
- Children's BaZi Analysis
- Family BaZi Analysis

Strategic Analysis for Corporate Organizations
- Corporate BaZi Consultations
- BaZi Analysis for Human Resource Management

Entrepreneurs & Business Owners
- BaZi Analysis for Entrepreneurs

Career Pursuits
- BaZi Career Analysis

Relationships
- Marriage and Compatibility Analysis
- Partnership Analysis

For Everyone
- Annual BaZi Forecast
- Your Personal BaZi Coach

Date Selection Consultations

- **Marriage Date Selection**
- **Caesarean Birth Date Selection**
- **House-Moving Date Selection**
- **Renovation & Groundbreaking Dates**
- **Signing of Contracts**
- **Official Openings**
- **Product Launches**

Corporate Events

Many reputable organizations and instituitions have worked closely with Joey Yap Consulting Group to build a synergistic business relationship by engaging our team of consultants, led by Joey Yap, as speakers at their corporate events.

We tailor our seminars and talks to suit the anticipated or pertinent group of audience. Be it department, subsidiary, your clients or even the entire corporation, we aim to fit your requirements in delivering the intended message(s).

Tel: +603-2284 1213   Email: consultation@joeyyap.com

Chinese Metaphysics Reference Series

The Chinese Metaphysics Reference Series is a collection of reference texts, source material, and educational textbooks to be used as supplementary guides by scholars, students, researchers, teachers and practitioners of Chinese Metaphysics.

These comprehensive and structured books provide fast, easy reference to aid in the study and practice of various Chinese Metaphysics subjects including Feng Shui, BaZi, Yi Jing, Zi Wei, Liu Ren, Ze Ri, Ta Yi, Qi Men and Mian Xiang.

The Chinese Metaphysics Compendium

At over 1,000 pages, the *Chinese Metaphysics Compendium* is a unique one-volume reference book that compiles all the formulas relating to Feng Shui, BaZi (Four Pillars of Destiny), Zi Wei (Purple Star Astrology), Yi Jing (I-Ching), Qi Men (Mystical Doorways), Ze Ri (Date Selection), Mian Xiang (Face Reading) and other sources of Chinese Metaphysics.

It is presented in the form of easy-to-read tables, diagrams and reference charts, all of which are compiled into one handy book. This first-of-its-kind compendium is presented in both English and the original Chinese, so that none of the meanings and contexts of the technical terminologies are lost.

The only essential and comprehensive reference on Chinese Metaphysics, and an absolute must-have for all students, scholars, and practitioners of Chinese Metaphysics.

The Ten Thousand Year Calendar (Pocket Edition)

The Ten Thousand Year Calendar

Dong Gong Date Selection

The Date Selection Compendium

Plum Blossoms Divination Reference Book

San Yuan Dragon Gate Eight Formations Water Method

Xuan Kong Da Gua Ten Thousand Year Calendar

Bazi Hour Pillar Useful Gods - Wood

Bazi Hour Pillar Useful Gods - Fire

Bazi Hour Pillar Useful Gods - Earth

Bazi Hour Pillar Useful Gods - Metal

Bazi Hour Pillar Useful Gods - Water

Xuan Kong Da Gua Structures Reference Book

Xuan Kong Da Gua 64 Gua Transformation Analysis

Bazi Structures and Structural Useful Gods - Wood

Bazi Structures and Structural Useful Gods - Fire

Bazi Structures and Structural Useful Gods - Earth

Bazi Structures and Structural Useful Gods - Metal

Bazi Structures and Structural Useful Gods - Water

Xuan Kong Purple White Script

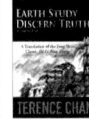
Earth Study Discern Truth Second Edition

www.masteryacademy.com | +603 - 2284 8080

Joey Yap's BaZi Profiling System

Three Levels of BaZi Profiling (English & Chinese versions)

In BaZi Profiling, there are three levels that reflect three different stages of a person's personal nature and character structure.

Level 1 – The Day Master

The Day Master in a nutshell is the BASIC YOU. The inborn personality. It is your essential character. It answers the basic question "WHO AM I". There are ten basic personality profiles – the TEN Day Masters – each with its unique set of personality traits, likes and dislikes.

Level 2 – The Structure

The Structure is your behavior and attitude – in other words, how you use your personality. It expands on the Day Master (Level 1). The structure reveals your natural tendencies in life – are you more controlling, more of a creator, supporter, thinker or connector? Each of the Ten Day Masters express themselves differently through the FIVE Structures. Why do we do the things we do? Why do we like the things we like? – The answers are in our BaZi STRUCTURE.

Level 3 – The Profile

The Profile reveals your unique abilities and skills, the masks that you consciously and unconsciously "put on" as you approach and navigate the world. Your Profile speaks of your ROLES in life. There are TEN roles – or Ten BaZi Profiles. Everyone plays a different role.

What makes you happy and what does success mean to you is different to somebody else. Your sense of achievement and sense of purpose in life is unique to your Profile. Your Profile will reveal your unique style.

The path of least resistance to your success and wealth can only be accessed once you get into your "flow." Your BaZi Profile reveals how you can get FLOW. It will show you your patterns in work, relationship and social settings. Being AWARE of these patterns is your first step to positive Life Transformation.

www.baziprofiling.com

BaZi Collections

Leading Chinese Astrology Master Trainer Joey Yap makes it easy to learn how to unlock your Destiny through your BaZi with these books. BaZi or Four Pillars of Destiny is an ancient Chinese science which enables individuals to understand their personality, hidden talents and abilities as well as their luck cycle, simply by examining the information contained within their birth data.

Understand and appreciate more about this astoundingly accurate ancient Chinese Metaphysical science with this BaZi Collection.

Feng Shui Collection

Must-Haves for Property Analysis!

For homeowners, those looking to build their own home or even investors who are looking to apply Feng Shui to their homes, these series of books provides valuable information from the classical Feng Shui therioes and applications.

In his trademark straight-to-the-point manner, Joey shares with you the Feng Shui do's and dont's when it comes to finding a property with favorable Feng Shui, which is condusive for home living.

Stories & Lessons on Feng Shui Series

All in all, this series is a delightful chronicle of Joey's articles, thoughts and vast experience - as a professional Feng Shui consultant and instructor - that have been purposely refined, edited and expanded upon to make for a light-hearted, interesting yet educational read. And with Feng Shui, BaZi, Mian Xiang and Yi Jing all thrown into this one dish, there's something for everyone.

   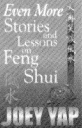

www.masteryacademy.com | +603 - 2284 8080

Continue Your Journey with Joey Yap Books in Feng Shui

Pure Feng Shui
Pure Feng Shui is Joey Yap's debut with an international publisher, CICO Books, and is a refreshing and elegant look at the intricacies of Classical Feng Shui – now compiled in a useful manner for modern-day readers. This book is a comprehensive introduction to all the important precepts and techniques of Feng Shui practice.

Your Aquarium Here
This book is the first in Fengshuilogy Series, a series of matter-in-fact and useful Feng Shui books designed for the person who wants to do a fuss-free Feng Shui.

Xuan Kong Flying Stars
This book is an essential introductory book to the subject of Xuan Kong Fei Xing, a well-known and popular system of Feng Shui. Learn 'tricks of the trade' and 'trade secrets' to enhance and maximize Qi in your home or office.

Walking the Dragons
Compiled in one book for the first time from Joey Yap's Feng Shui Mastery Excursion Series, the book highlights China's extensive, vibrant history with astute observations on the Feng Shui of important sites and places. Learn the landform formations of Yin Houses (tombs and burial places), as well as mountains, temples, castles, and villages.

The Art of Date Selection: Personal Date Selection
With the *Art of Date Selection: Personal Date Selection*, learn simple, practical methods you can employ to select not just good dates, but personalized good dates. Whether it's a personal activity such as a marriage or professional endeavor such as launching a business, signing a contract or even acquiring assets, this book will show you how to pick the good dates and tailor them to suit the activity in question, as well as avoid the negative ones too!

www.masteryacademy.com | +603 - 2284 8080

Face Reading Collection

Discover Face Reding (English & Chinese versions)

This is a comprehensive book on all areas of Face Reading, covering some of the most important facial features, including the forehead, mouth, ears and even philtrum above your lips. This book eill help you analyse not just your Destiny but help you achieve your full potential and achieve life fulfillment.

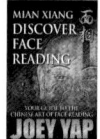 

Joey Yap's Art of Face Reading

The Art of Face Reading is Joey Yap's second effort with CICO Books, and takes a lighter, more practical approach to Face Reading. This book does not so much focus on the individual features as it does on reading the entire face. It is about identifying common personality types and characters.

Easy Guide on Face Reading (English & Chinese versions)

The Face Reading Essentials series of books comprises 5 individual books on the key features of the face – Eyes, Eyebrows, Ears, Nose, and Mouth. Each book provides a detailed illustration and a simple yet descriptive explanation on the individual types of the features.

The books are equally useful and effective for beginners, enthusiasts, and the curious. The series is designed to enable people who are new to Face Reading to make the most of first impressions and learn to apply Face Reading skills to understand the personality and character of friends, family, co-workers, and even business associates.

Annual Releases
2011 Annual Outlook & Tong Shu

Chinese Astrology for 2011   Feng Shui for 2011   Tong Shu Desktop Calendar 2011   Professional Tong Shu Diary 2011   Tong Shu Monthly Planner 2011   Weekly Tong Shu Diary 2011

www.masteryacademy.com | +603 - 2284 8080

Educational Tools and Software

Xuan Kong Flying Stars Feng Shui Software
The Essential Application for Enthusiasts and Professionals

The Xuan Kong Flying Stars Feng Shui Software will assist you in the practice of Xuan Kong Feng Shui with minimum fuss and maximum effectiveness. Superimpose the Flying Stars charts over your house plans (or those of your clients) to clearly demarcate the 9 Palaces. Use it to help you create fast and sophisticated chart drawings and presentations, as well as to assist professional practitioners in the report-writing process before presenting the final reports for your clients. Students can use it to practice their Xuan Kong Feng Shui skills and knowledge, and it can even be used by designers and architects!

BaZi Ming Pan Software Version 2.0
Professional Four Pillars Calculator for Destiny Analysis

The BaZi Ming Pan Version 2.0 Professional Four Pillars Calculator for Destiny Analysis is the most technically advanced software of its kind in the world today. It allows even those without any knowledge of BaZi to generate their own BaZi Charts, and provides virtually every detail required to undertake a comprehensive Destiny Analysis.

This Professional Four Pillars Calculator allows you to even undertake a day-to-day analysis of your Destiny. What's more, all BaZi Charts generated by this software are fully printable and configurable! Designed for both enthusiasts and professional practitioners, this state-of-the-art software blends details with simplicity, and is capable of generating 4 different types of BaZi charts: **BaZi Professional Charts, BaZi Annual Analysis Charts, BaZi Pillar Analysis Charts and BaZi Family Relationship Charts.**

Joey Yap Feng Shui Template Set

Directions are the cornerstone of any successful Feng Shui audit or application. The **Joey Yap Feng Shui Template Set** is a set of three templates to simplify the process of taking directions and determining locations and positions, whether it's for a building, a house, or an open area such as a plot of land, all with just a floor plan or area map.

The Set comprises 3 basic templates: The Basic Feng Shui Template, 8 Mansions Feng Shui Template, and the Flying Stars Feng Shui Template.

Mini Feng Shui Compass

The Mini Feng Shui Compass is a self-aligning compass that is not only light at 100gms but also built sturdily to ensure it will be convenient to use anywhere. The rings on the Mini Feng Shui Compass are bi-lingual and incorporate the 24 Mountain Rings that is used in your traditional Luo Pan.

The comprehensive booklet included will guide you in applying the 24 Mountain Directions on your Mini Feng Shui Compass effectively and the 8 Mansions Feng Shui to locate the most auspicious locations within your home, office and surroundings. You can also use the Mini Feng Shui Compass when measuring the direction of your property for the purpose of applying Flying Stars Feng Shui.

---

www.masteryacademy.com | +603 - 2284 8080

Educational Tools and Software

Xuan Kong Vol.1
An Advanced Feng Shui Home Study Course

Learn the Xuan Kong Flying Star Feng Shui system in just 20 lessons! Joey Yap's specialised notes and course work have been written to enable distance learning without compromising on the breadth or quality of the syllabus. Learn at your own pace with the same material students in a live class would use. The most comprehensive distance learning course on Xuan Kong Flying Star Feng Shui in the market. Xuan Kong Flying Star Vol.1 comes complete with a special binder for all your course notes.

Feng Shui for Period 8 - (DVD)

Don't miss the Feng Shui Event of the next 20 years! Catch Joey Yap LIVE and find out just what Period 8 is all about. This DVD boxed set zips you through the fundamentals of Feng Shui and the impact of this important change in the Feng Shui calendar. Joey's entertaining, conversational style walks you through the key changes that Period 8 will bring and how to tap into Wealth Qi and Good Feng Shui for the next 20 years.

Xuan Kong Flying Stars Beginners Workshop - (DVD)

Take a front row seat in Joey Yap's Xuan Kong Flying Stars workshop with this unique LIVE RECORDING of Joey Yap's Xuan Kong Flying Stars Feng Shui workshop, attended by over 500 people. This DVD program provides an effective and quick introduction of Xuan Kong Feng Shui essentials for those who are just starting out in their study of classical Feng Shui. Learn to plot your own Flying Star chart in just 3 hours. Learn 'trade secret' methods, remedies and cures for Flying Stars Feng Shui. This boxed set contains 3 DVDs and 1 workbook with notes and charts for reference.

BaZi Four Pillars of Destiny Beginners Workshop - (DVD)

Ever wondered what Destiny has in store for you? Or curious to know how you can learn more about your personality and inner talents? BaZi or Four Pillars of Destiny is an ancient Chinese science that enables us to understand a person's hidden talent, inner potential, personality, health and wealth luck from just their birth data. This specially compiled DVD set of Joey Yap's BaZi Beginners Workshop provides a thorough and comprehensive introduction to BaZi. Learn how to read your own chart and understand your own luck cycle. This boxed set contains 3 DVDs and 1 workbook with notes and reference charts.

www.masteryacademy.com | +603 - 2284 8080

DVD Series

Joey Yap's Face Reading Revealed DVD Series

Mian Xiang, the Chinese art of Face Reading, is an ancient form of physiognomy and entails the use of the face and facial characteristics to evaluate key aspects of a person's life, luck and destiny. In his Face Reading DVDs series, Joey Yap shows you how the facial features reveal a wealth of information about a person's luck, destiny and personality.

Mian Xiang also tell us the talents, quirks and personality of an individual. Do you know that just by looking at a person's face, you can ascertain his or her health, wealth, relationships and career? Let Joey Yap show you how the 12 Palaces can be utilised to reveal a person's inner talents, characteristics and much more.

Feng Shui for Homebuyers DVD Series

In these DVDs, you will also learn how to identify properties with good Feng Shui features that will help you promote a fulfilling life and achieve your full potential. Discover how to avoid properties with negative Feng Shui that can bring about detrimental effects to your health, wealth and relationships.

Joey will also elaborate on how to fix the various aspects of your home that may have an impact on the Feng Shui of your property and give pointers on how to tap into the positive energies to support your goals.

Discover Feng Shui with Joey Yap: Set of 4 DVDs
Informative and entertaining, classical Feng Shui comes alive in *Discover Feng Shui with Joey Yap!*

You have the questions. Now let Joey personally answer them in this 4-set DVD compilation! Learn how to ensure the viability of your residence or workplace, Feng Shui-wise, without having to convert it into a Chinese antiques' shop. Classical Feng Shui is about harnessing the natural power of your environment to improve quality of life. It's a systematic and subtle metaphysical science.

Walking the Dragons with Joey Yap (The TV Series)

This DVD set features eight episodes, covering various landform Feng Shui analyses and applications from Joey Yap as he and his co-hosts travel through China. It includes case studies of both modern and historical sites with a focus on Yin House (burial places) Feng Shui and the tombs of the Qing Dynasty emperors.

The series was partly filmed on-location in mainland China, and the state of Selangor, Malaysia.

www.masteryacademy.com | +603 - 2284 8080

Home Study Courses

Gain Valuable Knowledge from the Comfort of Your Home

Now, armed with your trusty computer or laptop and Internet access, knowledge of Chinese Metaphysics is just a click away!

3 easy steps to activate your Home Study Course:

Step 1:
Go to the URL as indicated on the Activation Card, and key in your Activation Code

Step 2:
At the Registration page, fill in the details accordingly to enable us to generate your Student Identification (Student ID).

Step 3:
Upon successful registration, you may begin your lessons immediately.

Joey Yap's Feng Shui Mastery HomeStudy Course

Module 1: **Empowering Your Home**
Module 2: **Master Practitioner Program**

Learn how easy it is to harness the power of the environment to promote health, wealth and prosperity in your life. The knowledge and applications of Feng Shui will no more be a mystery but a valuable tool you can master on your own.

Joey Yap's BaZi Mastery HomeStudy Course

Module 1: **Mapping Your Life**
Module 2: **Mastering Your Future**

Discover your path of least resistance to success with insights about your personality and capabilities, and what strengths you can tap on to maximize your potential for success and happiness by mastering BaZi (Chinese Astrology). This course will teach you all the essentials you need to interpret a BaZi chart and more.

Joey Yap's Mian Xiang Mastery HomeStudy Course

Module 1: **Face Reading**
Module 2: **Advanced Face Reading**

A face can reveal so much about a person. Now, you can learn the art and science of Mian Xiang (Chinese Face Reading) to understand a person's character based on his or her facial features with ease and confidence.

www.masteryacademy.com | +603 - 2284 8080

Feng Shui Mastery™
LIVE COURSES (MODULES ONE TO FOUR)

The Feng Shui Mastery™ comprises Feng Shui Mastery Modules 1, 2, 3 and 4. It starts off with a foundation program up to the advanced practitioner level. It is a thorough, comprehensive program that covers important theories from various classical Feng Shui systems including Ba Zhai, San Yuan, San He, and Xuan Kong.

Module One: Beginners Course   **Module Two:** Practitioners Course   **Module Three:** Advanced Practitioners Course   **Module Four:** Master Course

BaZi Mastery™
LIVE COURSES (MODULES ONE TO FOUR)

The BaZi Mastery™ consists of BaZi Mastery Modules 1, 2, 3 and 4. In Modules 1 and 2, students will receive a thorough introduction to BaZi, along with an intensive understanding of BaZi principles and the requisite skills to practice it with accuracy and precision. This will prepare them, and serious Feng Shui practitioners, for a more advanced levels and fine-tune their application skills in Modules 3 and 4.

Module One: Intensive Foundation Course   **Module Two:** Practitioners Course   **Module Three:** Advanced Practitioners Course   **Module Four:** Master Course in BaZi

Xuan Kong Mastery™
LIVE COURSES (MODULES ONE TO THREE)
* Advanced Courses For Master Practitioners

The Xuan Kong Mastery™ comprises Xuan Kong Mastery Modules 1, 2A, 2B and 3. It is a sophisticated branch of Feng Shui replete with many techniques and formulae, enabling practitioners to evaluate Feng Shui on a more thorough and in-depth basis. The study of Xuan Kong encompasses numerology, symbology and science of the Ba Gua along with the mathematics of time.

Module One: Advanced Foundation Course   **Module Two A:** Advanced Xuan Kong Methodologies   **Module Two B:** Purple White   **Module Three:** Advanced Xuan Kong 'Da Gua

www.masteryacademy.com | +603 - 2284 8080

Mian Xiang Mastery™
LIVE COURSES (MODULES ONE AND TWO)

The Mian Xiang Mastery™ comprises of Mian Xiang Mastery Modules 1 and 2 to allow students to learn this ancient art in a thorough, detailed manner. Each module has a carefully-developed syllabus that allows students to get acquainted with the fundamentals of Mian Xiang before moving on to the more intricate theories and principles that will enable them to practice Mian Xiang with greater depth and complexity.

Module One:
Basic Face Reading

Module Two:
Practical Face Reading

Yi Jing Mastery™
LIVE COURSES (MODULES ONE AND TWO)

The Yi Jing Mastery™ comprises Modules 1 and 2. Both Modules aim to give casual and serious Yi Jing enthusiasts a serious insight into one of the most important philosophical treatises in ancient Chinese thought. Yi Jing uses sophisticated formulas and calculations to derive the answers to questions we pose. It is a science of divination, and in our classes there is a heavy emphasis on the scientific aspect of it. It bears no religious or superstitious affiliation.

Module One:
Traditional Yi Jing

Module Two:
Plum Blossom Numerology

Ze Ri Mastery™
LIVE COURSES (MODULES ONE AND TWO)

The ZeRi Mastery™ consists of ZeRi Mastery Modules 1 and 2. This program provides students with a thorough introduction to the art of Date Selection both for Personal and Feng Shui purposes. Our ZeRi Mastery™ aims to provide a thorough and comprehensive program on the art of Date Selection, covering everything from Personal and Feng Shui Date Selection to Xuan Kong Da Gua Date Selection.

Module One:
Personal and Feng Shui Date Selection

Module Two:
Xuan Kong Da Gua Date Selection

www.masteryacademy.com | +603 - 2284 8080